Dem

C000180245

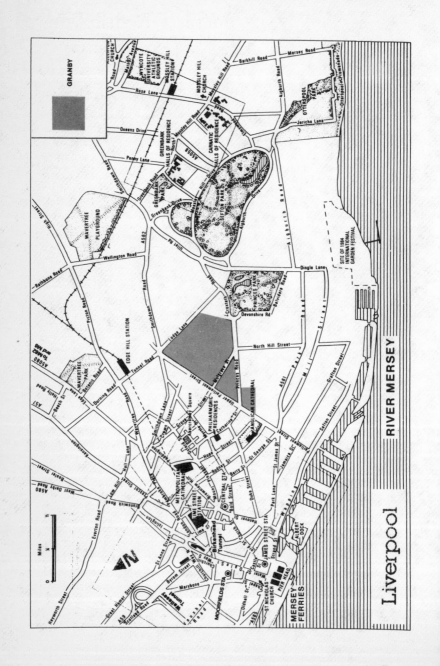

Liverpool

RIVER MERSEY

Democracy Rediscovered:

A STUDY IN POLICE ACCOUNTABILITY

Margaret Simey

Pluto  Press

First published 1988 by Pluto Publishing Ltd
11-21 Northdown Street, London N1 9BN

Distributed in the USA by Allen & Unwin Inc.
8 Winchester Place
Winchester
MA 01890, USA

Copyright © Margaret Simey 1988

Printed and bound in the United Kingdom by
Billing & Son Ltd, Worcester

All rights reserved

**British Library Cataloguing in Publication
Data**

Simey, Margaret
    Police accountability.
1. Merseyside Police
I. Title
363.2'09427'5   HV8196.A5M4

ISBN 0−7453−0262−9
ISBN 0−7453−0277−7 Pbk

Contents

Glossary

AMA   Association of Metropolitan Authorities
ACPO   Association of Chief Police Officers
ACLO   Assistant Community Liaison Officer
NRC   National Reporting Centre
SNAP   Shelter Neighbourhood Action Project
CIPFA   Chartered Institute of Public Finance and Accountancy

The Police Committee was set up by the County Council to act as a **Police Authority**. As an Authority its powers were derived directly from statute and were not delegated by the County Council. The Metropolitan County Council was abolished in 1986 when the Authority was replaced by a Joint Board.

The 'Big Mets' was the name popularly used in reference to the six Metropolitan County Councils (Greater Manchester, West Midlands, South Yorkshire, West Yorkshire, Tyne and Wear, Merseyside.)

Toxteth Section. The name commonly used in referring to the intensive beat project initiated in the Toxteth area in January 1982.

Introduction

Are our inner cities ungovernable? Are the forces of law and order doomed to defeat before the advancing hordes of the new urban barbarism? Are the police in control — or out of it? A decade ago few would have thought of asking these questions. The very fact that such doubts and fears are put into words and openly discussed by the media is a measure of the extent to which concern as to where we now stand has developed in recent years. They raise issues of fundamental importance. Is policing by consent and, by implication, government by consent, a practical possibility in the complex society of the post-industrial era? Is democracy a lost cause and must the people of the inner cities resign themselves to their new status as urban colonists subject to government by remote control? Is riot and revolution and its repression by force the only answer? Each question triggers off another till the head spins and the heart falters before the complexity and magnitude of the problems which demand solution. The massive support for a third term of a national government whose philosophy permits them to ride rough-shod over those principles of social responsibility on which democracy depends can but add to the foreboding as to the future.

Faced with such questions in the context of Liverpool in the 1980s it is difficult to do other than despair. The unseemly abuse of power in recent years by the Militants, the abolition of the Merseyside County Council and with it the Police Authority, the deepening despondency in the inner city as the walls of the ghetto of deprivation become ever more tangible, are witness to the decay of the entire system of government as I have known it. I hate to think that in my five years as Chairman of the Merseyside Police Authority I should have presided over a decline in democratic practice such as I could never have thought possible in so short a time. The abolition of the six 'Big Mets' (the Metropolitan Police Authorities) marked a point of no return on the road to Ulster so far as policing by consent was concerned. The Joint Boards which succeeded them constitute a return of responsibility to the judiciary which puts the clock back by a century. The benevolent paternalism of policing in the past has given way to bureaucratic control without accountability which is typical of the centralised government of today. Woe betide me that I should be held to account for such a state of affairs.

I represented the Granby ward in the heart of Toxteth for 23 years till 1986 without a break, first on the Liverpool City Council and later on the Merseyside County Council. For the last five years I was Chairman of the Merseyside Police Authority. Throughout that long stretch, I worked hard to the best of my ability. I sacrificed family and friends to politics, saw myself turn from a reasonably personable woman into a scraggy Grandma Buggins, angrier in old age than I ever was when young. Yet a bitter post-card circulated in the ward by a black media group shows a brick wall with the graffiti message 'They Haven't Done Nothing'. Has all I've striven for gone for naught?

Damned if I'll end my life on that weary note. If nothing else, I've lived, not vegetated. Not for nothing have I existed for 80 long years, survived two world wars, endured two major economic recessions, to make no mention of the sundry ups and downs which are the common lot of the human race. The obligation presses heavily upon me to shine my candle still. Maybe there is little to show for it all but I must surely have acquired some wisdom, learned some lessons, that I can pass on to those who follow. Because I can see so far into the past, can it be that I have found — not the truth; that would be too extravagant a claim — but some clue to the way forward? I must surely have some gift, however small, to offer to the next generation.

I am buoyed up in this endeavour by the memory of the delight with which I was welcomed by the Basuoto community for whom my son worked in Lesotho. How exceptionally fortunate he was to have such a very old mother, they exclaimed. To them, to have access to the wisdom of a long life was as valuable as cash in the bank. I remember, too, the Chief Constable who encountered me in the flesh for the first time at a conference. 'Why, she's nothing like what she's made out to be,' he exclaimed in astonishment. This is my opportunity to vindicate what has so often been misrepresented as reckless and subversive behaviour on my part. It is in that spirit that I put pen to paper. I am accountable for the life that I have lived. I have been no helpless puppet or factory robot. All my life I have been privileged to enjoy a freedom of choice as to how I should spend my days which is denied to very many people. What have I to say for myself?

Though I trust that experience has brought me to a duly humble state of mind, it has done nothing to lessen my commitment to the principles of democracy to which I was born and in which I was brought up. On the contrary, the flame of my conviction now blazes all the more brightly because of the encircling gloom. Never can there have been greater need for a declaration of faith in the right of every individual to a fair share in the responsibility for the management of our common affairs. It is the deprivation of that right which lies at the root of the breakdown of law and order that blights our times. The loneliness and insecurity of which we so loudly complain are the inevitable fate of a people dedicated to the pursuit of blinkered self-interest. To turn a tide of such fearsome strength calls for courage and conviction. It is the reward of a long life that the more the battle seems to go against all that I stand for, the more convinced I am that victory can and must be won. I am a born again democrat. It is my hope that by telling the story of how my own commitment to democratic government has reached its present intensity I may be able to share with others something of the vision I have of the future and so encourage them to face these difficult times with greater resolution. I describe that pilgrimage in terms of my experience as an elected member for the Granby ward because it is to the people of Toxteth that I owe such political sensibility and wisdom as I may have achieved. It is thanks to them that though I regard the future with an acute awareness of the immensity of the task ahead of us, I do so with a renewed conviction that democracy can and must survive in the New World which we are now entering. It is in that belief that I offer this, my last will and testament as a politician.

Following the abolition of the Merseyside County Council in 1986, I could have used my new-found leisure to 'spill the beans' about life behind the scenes during the stormy years of my Chairmanship of the Merseyside Police Authority. The fear of libel actions would have spoiled the fun though the media would doubtless have enjoyed it. That apart, the predicament in which we find ourselves today rules out the possibility of laughter. A certain freedom of speech is appropriate to one who has retired from the fray but laughter dies on my lips. Did Cassandra ever smile, I wonder, as she ran through the streets crying doom and disaster? Instead, what I offer is simply an account of how one small group of elected representatives struggled to get to grips with the problems of government in an urban society so far as a single public service, that of policing, was concerned. It was an endeavour which led us into deep waters. Can democracy work in a conurbation and if so how, in the most practical of terms, is this to be done? How can a public service manned by professionals be 'controlled' by the people it exists to serve? Is the intrusion of 'politics' a threat to sound administration? This book is about how we on the Merseyside Police Authority came to ask such questions and to what conclusions the search for answers forced us to come.

What emerged with stunning clarity out of all the fog and confusion surrounding the riots of 1981 was that a chasm of devastating dimensions had opened up between police and policed, a gulf so wide that the sole means of communication across it was by the beating of plastic shields and the throwing of milk bottle bombs. It was only when we began to probe more deeply that the wider implications of that discovery came to be realised. What the inquiry we instituted revealed was that the gulf was due to no mere inadequacy in the exchange of news and views but to a flaw in the relationship between the two sides so profound as to endanger the validity of the entire service. Set in this context, the designation of all those in authority in whatever capacity as 'Them' and those who are subject to that authority as 'Us' is no flippant cocking of a snook but a statement of fact of the greatest significance. As the riots demonstrated, the consequences of such a separation are disastrous. 'Government' is by imposition, not consent. Now that I have time to reflect, it is clear to me that the ultimate lesson of the dreadful experiences of the riots, and indeed, of the whole long span of my political life, is simply this, that times have changed but political practice has stood still. We have failed, and failed lamentably, to adapt the democratic principles to which we declare our allegiance to the circumstances in which we now find ourselves. Our masters no longer speak the language of the people. As a Scouser wit has put it, it is not Toxteth that is a problem for the government but government that is a problem for Toxteth.

Our exploration of this situation may have been small in scale and narrow in focus but I believe that the discoveries we made are straws which can serve the invaluable purpose of indicating which way the wind blows. The lessons we learned were more important than anything tangible which we as a Police Authority achieved or failed to achieve. Through trial and tribulation we reached the point where we began to sense some solid ground of principle beneath our feet on which to build the new structure of government which the future requires of us. This record has been prepared in the belief that the outcome of our experience is of direct relevance to the difficult transition from the industrialisation of the past into the obscurity of the future which we are now undergoing. What has befallen Merseyside is no unique destiny reserved for us alone but undoubtedly one which lies ahead for the country as a whole.

It was no mere chance that it was Merseyside that chose to tackle this issue with particular vigour. The common experience of the times has always taken on a larger-than-life dimension in the Liverpool context: we only shout more loudly because the shoe pinches more painfully in our case. It is our perverse boast that the search for original solutions which is characteristic of the Liverpool story has been inspired by exceptional necessity. More than most, we have been at the mercy of the slings and arrows of outrageous fortune, quite literally dependent on the fluctuations of wind and weather. Sometimes these have brought great wealth, as the monumental river front of the Pierhead bears witness; sometimes rich and poor alike have suffered from the vagaries of dependence on the international commercial system based on credit.

True to form, the disturbances of 1981 revealed a state of decline in Merseyside far in advance of that in any other part of the country. Just as at one time we were in the van of industrial progress, so now we are in the forefront of the plunge into the obscurity of an unknown future. The riots were a melodramatic presentation of the fact that the entire fabric of our daily lives, be it economic, social or even moral, is undergoing irreversible change. Multiple stress has become a problem in its own right. The unemployed not only suffer as individuals but by their very number constitute far too high a proportion of the population for any community to carry. The riots were a bitter protest against the reduction of a whole community to a state of intolerable dependency.

Added to this, Liverpool has always lacked the foundations of a traditional stability which fortified other towns when they were subjected to the stress of rapid change. Throughout the entire period of its mushroom growth as a boom city in the nineteenth century, its population has been bolstered by successive cargoes of migrants who sought escape from poverty and oppression in their native lands. It is ironic that one of the most recent should have come from the West Indies, descendants of the victims of the trade in human beings on which the city's early fortunes were founded.

The city has developed a character which is a direct reflection of its origins. It still bears the hallmarks of a vast transit camp. The people are survivors born and bred, quick to turn their deprivations to their own advantage. Theirs is a way of life which rouses in those who encounter it simultaneous envy and exasperation. The constant through-flow of newcomers renders doubly elusive that state which Scarman called public tranquillity. A brutal environment has bred a brutal response. There is a long tradition of violent protest as the last resort of those whose lack of education or of opportunity denied them any other means of securing the remedy of their just grievances. Ours was the one police force which went on strike in 1919. It is not without significance that it is here that Militancy, that defiance of traditional custom and practice, should take root.

Bearing all this in mind it was surely not fortuitous that the focus of our concern should be policing. The immediate lesson of the disturbances in Toxteth in 1981 was that our troubles stemmed from the gap between police and policed but this concealed the fact of the even wider separation of 'Them' from 'Us', government from governed. The roots of the city's problems lie deep in the past but those who govern have been slow to recognise our need, all too quick to declare us a 'problem' and blind to the frailty of a community buffetted almost beyond endurance. If in these circumstances we are to achieve policing by consent it can only be with the support and co-operation of the people concerned. But how is this to be achieved when there is on the one hand, massive disillusionment with the customary democratic procedures and on the other, an unassailable rejection of the principle of accountability?

Lacking the support of the people, those in authority turn to the law for vindication of what they seek to do. With increasing frequency and ever-rising stridency, the police are called upon to deal with the consequences of the breakdown of government which lies at the root of our difficulties. When inevitably they fail to achieve the impossible demands made upon them, the blame is put on them. Meanwhile, vandalism, petty crime and worse may be only the symptoms of a deeper malaise but they must be contained and the task of containment brings with it special difficulties with and for the police. These in turn impose an immense strain upon the machinery within which the police force operates. The fact is, as we discovered to our considerable consternation, that it is in regard to policing that the breakdown of democratic practice has been taken to its most frightening extreme. In no other public service has the takeover of control by the executive been so complete, the extrusion of the public so thoroughgoing. Perhaps even more alarming, as I learned from painful experience, when critics voice concern that this should be so, the public dare not listen for fear that this last bastion of security might also be revealed as deficient. When we set out to try to rectify this wholly unacceptable state of affairs, the embargo on 'political interference' was total. To make our position even more difficult, the Metropolitan Police Authorities were new cogs in the machinery of government when they were set up in 1974. We therefore started from scratch. We had to invent a reason for our own existence and justify it by our own deeds. If the going as I have presented it sometimes seems slow, it is because the pioneering of strange territory is inevitably an affair of fits and starts, trial and error. Until we set out in search of accountability, few people had gone beyond armchair theorising.

The book falls into three parts. The first sets the scene against which the drama is played out. Granby was and is typical of any inner city area. In it live the people the management of whose common affairs — or the failure to manage — is the nub of the matter. In the 23 years I served as one of their elected representatives I witnessed the gradual alienation of the whole community from the society of which they were a part. My use of the word ghetto may cause offence to some by reason of its association with racism but no other word so aptly conveys the feeling which inspired the constant cry of 'We are forgotten people'. Locked in a downward spiral of social disintegration not of their own making and unmerited by any fault on their part, they found themselves denied either the means of escape or redress of their grievances. The apparent indifference of those in authority gave rise to frustration and hostility of which the police inevitably bore the brunt.

In the second part I move to the other side of the counter, giving in considerable detail what might at first sight appear to be a straightforward account of how a Police Authority works. This could be criticised as being a specialist subject which should have been the material of a quite different book. In fact, as we ourselves learned, it was precisely that assumption, that policing is nothing to do with ordinary people, that had brought about the breakdown in the relationship between police and public in Granby. The unexpected outcome of the close attention we paid to the operational activities of the Force was, therefore, that we came to realise that we were aiming at the wrong target: it was to the resolution of the problem of the gap between 'Them' and 'Us' that our energies should be directed. Effective accountability was surely the answer but our every endeavour to achieve this seemed doomed to failure. The dilemma we faced was how to combine the necessity to delegate authority with the essential need to retain ultimate responsibility in the hands of the people. Our five years in office were directed to the search for a resolution of that dilemma. To this, I believe, we made a valuable contribution.

In the third part, I describe how, to my surprise, it became apparent at the end of the day that our concern had not been with the police but with the problems of government in an urban conurbation. The police service may be special in certain respects but it is in no way separable or different from the political structure in general. This chapter therefore attempts to set our experience as a Police Authority in the context of the urban crisis in general.

The underlying theme throughout the book has been that of the gulf between 'Them' and 'Us'. We are not governed by consent but by imposition. It is the alienation of the people from their government that is at the roots of our present predicament. How is this to be remedied? Political will is called for.

The right to work, and the improvement of the conditions of the workers used to be the moral imperative which inspired political action. It is no longer valid and may never be so again. The imperative of the future lies in finding some other means of ensuring the universal right of the individual to be a responsible member of the society in which we find ourselves. It is our common deprivation of that right which results in the social disintegration of today, and which denies the government the support of a stable society in which to operate. In the elimination of that universal deprivation lies the cure for the urban crisis and the hope for the future.

This is no academic study. A mass of literature is produced these days by researchers who buzz like bees round the honeypot of policing, inner cities, violence and other associated topics. Desirable though all this interest undoubtedly is, the results seldom reach either the public or those elected to represent their interests other than through the interpretation of the media. For me to present my story in the conventional language of the academic or the civil servant would contribute nothing to bridging this gulf. It is for that reason that I have made no reference to the work of other writers, greatly indebted though I am to many of them and to those in the media who bring to our attention material which would otherwise escape us. To underpin my argument with academic references to which the average reader has no access would defeat my object.

I hope that by the use of anecdote and personal experience I will succeed in arousing an interest in the principles and practice of government and an understanding of the way society moves down the road of social change among those who would be deterred by a more formal presentation. There are books galore about the theory of government and the working of Parliament but few descriptions of how it works at local level. There is no 'Yes, Minister' for local government. This is especially true so far as the police are concerned. Much of the argument about the 'control' of the police stems from sheer ignorance as to how a Police Authority works, what powers it has and what it can or cannot do.

The feeling that we were exploring the unknown characterised our entire existence as a Police Authority. We learned by doing. What we thought at any one time determined what we did then and there; experience taught us where our thinking had led us astray and vice versa. The process was one of continuous action and reaction to the circumstances of the day. It would be misleading to imply that we were at any time fully alert to the significance of what we were doing. The sense of purpose which I can now see underlay our activities, the discernible pattern of progress and the conscious interpretation of what we were doing, have only come with hindsight.

This is therefore no impartial and factual record of events. On the contrary it is essentially my own personal impression of what was going on all about me. Through no particular merit of my own, I happened to be in the right place at the right moment, in a key position which gave me an unrivalled opportunity to observe and comment. What I have tried to pin down on paper is what I felt and sensed, the hunches I had and the lessons I learned. Others, especially the police, may well deny the accuracy of my interpretation but this is how I saw it. I can only vouch for that truth.

One last word: I suffered from incessant allegations that all our troubles were due to personalities, either mine or that of Kenneth Oxford, the Chief Constable, or both of us together. This always crops up at question time whenever I speak at meetings of any kind. The Loveday Report (1985) dispels the claim that all was sweetness and light till I took the Chair but it would be foolish to deny that we both have strong personalities and like to have our own way. Nor that the worlds we lived in were totally different and communication across the gulf which separated us was a genuine difficulty. I know that my habitual irony was offensive to many policemen. And obviously, the free and easy challenge to authority in any shape or form by a Scouser politician, even when concealed behind what the media called my 'aristocratic manner', must have been hard for a top policeman to tolerate.

Which having been said, I must emphasise that our personal relationship was characterised by a curious and sometimes enjoyable sense of camaraderie. To perch at the top of the tree is always a lonely business and I think we were both on occasion glad to be able to share the tribulations of leadership with each other. I certainly respected the Chief's total commitment to his Force and to his profession however much I judged it to be excessive. When at intervals pressure from our respective followers forced us to joust in public like medieval knights, I like to think that neither of us took it personally. The argument between us concerned the dilemma of the conflict between professional autonomy and democratic control.

What I completely failed to grasp was the enormity of the gulf between my expectations and those of the Chief. My predecessor in the Chair, a Tory Councillor of long standing, had been prepared to accept that the police were an exception to local government custom and practice. He saw his job as being to give total and unquestioning support to the Force. With my socialist background and my personal philosophy, it never entered my head that such a stance was possible. I took it for granted that what was sauce for the goose of education or social services was equally appropriate for the gander of policing. Many of the strains and stresses which ensued could, I think, be attributed to my failure to spot that this gulf in understanding existed.

If the consequent conflict could have been attributed to the idiosyncracies of an individual, we might have shrugged it off as a burden we had to learn to carry; after all, we had appointed the Chief in the first place. As it was, some if not all of us were in absolutely no doubt that what confronted us was a conflict of issues which went far beyond personalities. It was against the system and what it stood for that our criticisms must be directed and not the manpower.

In conclusion I must pay tribute to that gallant regiment of family and friends, colleagues and Labour Party members, and all the patient listeners at endless meetings and conferences on whom I have been so dependent for stimulus and support through what were often rewarding but nevertheless dark and difficult days. Though they are too numerous to mention individually I owe a particular debt to those who helped me through the long toil of actually committing my thoughts to paper. I must make special reference to the Department of Continuing Education at the University of Liverpool which conferred on me the inestimable benefit of membership as an Honorary Fellow which did so much to counter the contempt with which the Merseyside Police Authority, and I along with it, were abolished.

Behind every Chairman is a Deputy on whom the quality of a committee's work largely depends but to whom credit is rarely attributed. I had the singular good fortune to find in George Bundred a Deputy of exceptional ability and expertise, as stalwart in his loyalty in times of stress as he was self-effacing when things went well. That he should become a personal friend was an unexpected and valued bonus.

It will be evident in the course of my story that a vital contribution to such progress as we made came from the team of administrators in the Merseyside County Council. We were exceptionally fortunate in having the services of a group of quite exceptional ability. The relationship we developed with them was a complete vindication of the viability of partnership between professional and politician as the basis of the democratic practice of government. The compulsory break-up of that team as a consequence of the abolition of the County Council was a waste of resources which is symptomatic of the malaise of centralism and little short of criminal.

As for the police, I can only reiterate the conviction which I tried to convey to them, so often in vain. It is not in the manpower that fault is to be found but in the dogmatism of the system which binds them hand and foot and causes some at least to deny the very principles which they personally hold most dear. This is the reason why I have throughout consistently referred to our chief officer by his title as Chief Constable and rarely by his name. Our target was the system not the individual. I must express my appreciation to those members of the Force who, though they might be baffled by my constant criticism, nevertheless paid me the compliment of accepting the sincerity of my intention.

It is no cliché to conclude with an attempt to express my gratitude to the people about whose lives and fortunes this book is written. By permitting me to become involved in their affairs they 'skinned my eyes' for me to the true meaning of much in life that would otherwise have passed me by. Their instinctive grasp of what democracy is about was for me the inspiration of my continuing commitment. Their strong sense of values is rooted deep in the truth of personal experience. If I talk of Granby as a 'ghetto of deprivation' it is no reflection on their character but of my own rage against the injustice which is inflicted upon a people in whose loyalty to the fundamentals of human decency lies our best hope for the future.

Part I

1

The Creation of a Ghetto

The Granby ward is a period piece. Situated at the heart of the urban sprawl that has come to be known as Toxteth, it exhibits all the afflictions of ageing. Disintegration of body and soul runs rampant through what used to be an eminently desirable neighbourhood, bound together by the anxious passion of the common commitment to respectability. A familiar enough story but being Liverpool, one which in the case of Granby takes on that element of exaggeration which is characteristic of the city. By chance, because of restrictions imposed on the use of land within the boundaries of King John's Forest of Toxteth, no building took place there till 1868. Then within two years, the entire area was developed in one fell swoop. This had the unforeseen consequence that a hundred years on, as we know to our cost, the whole estate and everything in it equally simultaneously reached the end of its useful life, creating a housing problem of unusual dimensions. It also accounts for the fact that it is possible to define the boundaries of the area with exceptional precision, a bonus for the urban sociologist but one which has borne exceptionally bitter fruit for its people.

Looking at it even now, with what remains of its wide and tree-lined streets, it still displays the remnants of the charm of the garden suburb it was evidently intended to be, though the term had not then been invented. A few major roads with large villas cut through street after street of small terrace houses. But however modest, these were not dwellings for the poor. Judging by the street registers of the day, many of the new residents must have been first generation white-collar people, eager to establish their difference from the mass of casual labourers. A single bush of privet by the front door; the tiniest of bow windows in the front room; a miniscule basement in which only the smallest of domestics could have existed; these bear witness to an overriding determination to achieve an improved social status. No industrial development of any kind was allowed to intrude. No pubs were permitted. Such bye-law housing as was built was concentrated at the top end of the ward, by the Lodge Lane which was to bring the neighbourhood into disrepute in 1981. Even there, the tenants adopted the general air of respectability though the houses were so tightly packed together as to make it possible to knock on two doors simultaneously when canvassing.

Respectability ruled supreme and continued to do so long after the first gloss of newness wore off. Till recently, there was still a baker's shop in Granby Street which displayed a Swiss confectioner's name above its door. The honours list in the Board School of which I am a Governor shows that the school regularly added to its academic successes. There were more churches to the mile of Princes Avenue, leading to Paxton's great park, than might have been thought necessary as a visible demonstration of the sanctity of the residents. Even the outbreak of the Second World War had little apparent effect and afterwards, though Corporation housing programmes brought new neighbours all around the borders, Granby itself remained an enclave of old-style order and law. In the paradoxical Liverpool tradition, it was long regarded as a Tory stronghold though this was indicative of loyalty to the Protestant faith rather than of satisfaction with the conditions of working life. Only in the corner by the Rialto Cinema was there cause for apprehension amongst the established residents: for self-evident reasons it was dubbed by ward members for leafletting purposes as the 'Black Square'.

Nevertheless after the Second World War the onset of old age inevitably brought about a quickening of the deterioration of the physical fabric. The tenants of the small houses in the side streets continued their struggle to maintain the standards of living to which they were accustomed: my own indifferent housekeeping has often been put to shame by the effort put into ensuring that at least the front room was always redecorated before Christmas. Not only were the drains and the water supply inadequate to meet the needs of the expanded population (there were still many houses with a linked water supply: while the first house filled a kettle, no one else could draw any water) but they were rapidly becoming beyond repair. Not a house escaped the universal blight of insufficient maintenance or the need for major rehabilitation. Modern morality will no longer tolerate the mixture of the sexes inevitable in a two-down and two-up or the misery of a WC in a cold back yard. Even the trees, once so pleasing, were now full grown giants which had, from lack of pruning, come to block out all the daylight in the adjacent houses.

The better off who lived in the bigger homes on the wide main streets had been the first to find themselves defeated by the struggle to maintain their old way of life. The threats of air-raids had speeded their departure. A fair number lingered on, left high and dry on a beach of loneliness, their families gone elsewhere, their houses far too big for their solitary needs. Life in a four-storey house with huge cold rooms, a single lavatory and ancient bathroom, a basement kitchen complete with a boiler for washing clothes and possibly a wine cellar, was simply too anachronistic to survive. They moved out if 'the Corpy' could rehouse them, or simply waited for death to pick them off, meanwhile uneasily taking in lodgers or letting rooms to eke out their resources.

It was these main streets which were to prove Granby's point of vulnerability to change. For the gradual process of decline was suddenly accelerated at the end of the 1950s when, after much political wrangling, the decision was taken to permit the clearance for development of the entire crown of Brownlow Hill. This unleashed the University's appetite for land. The Robbins Report in 1963 confirmed that the resources for expansion would be forthcoming. The area round Abercromby Square had originally been built to provide rather elegant town houses for the prosperous but the gathering momentum of the drift to the suburbs in the nineteenth century meant that it had come to serve as a refuge for a concentration of the rootless and the alienated who could find no other perch. It was there that I was myself introduced to the reality of extreme poverty when, as the University's first Social Science degree student in the 1920s, I was taken to visit a family living in one small room at the top of a wreck of a house. What I at first took to be a large doll lay on the table alongside such food as was available. In fact it was the corpse of a baby which the family were too poor to bury. Subsequently, Abercromby had served to accommodate the multi-racial population set adrift by the blitz on the dockside.

The intensity of the concentration of human difficulty in that particular area is vividly illustrated by the maps which accompany a survey of the distribution of 'social defects' undertaken in 1957 by my husband's Department of Social Science. Whatever the particular factor selected, it achieved its greatest density in Abercromby. The evacuation of such a conglomerate group of people at the University's behest proved far more difficult than had been anticipated. The students protested on behalf of those who suffered but in a city bereft of housing stock by the air-raids, the University could do no more than try. The city and the shopping areas blocked any movement to the east and north. There was neither space nor welcome for such a motley crowd in the solid bulk of the railway territory further up towards Edge Hill. All that was left was to go south, into Granby. And in Granby the vacuum left by the vacating of the bigger houses yawned wide. By the mid-1960s the whole population of Abercromby was on the move. Like a stream of refugees in a war film, the dispossessed trundled prams loaded with such gear as they called their own across Upper Parliament Street, their furniture on borrowed handcarts, and at their heels children, endless children.

The consequences were dramatic. If the survey had been repeated, how different the maps would have been. Although I had served my apprenticeship in the poorest parts of Scotland Road, never before had I encountered such a level of deprivation. Jam-packed with humanity, it was a case of individual survival. Amberley Street and Mulgrave Street were perfect examples. Lined with showy Victorian villas, they were the handiest for the migration from Abercromby. Every scrap of space was quickly occupied. What happened there was true of all the main streets. For lack of maintenance and modernisation the roofs leaked, the plumbing was antiquated, the water supply pathetic, the gas installation a museum piece and the electricity minimal and dangerous. The only bidders at that time were smart operators able to lay hands on ready cash, indifferent to the fact that the lease had only 10 or 20 years to run. They knew that at the rents they could charge, they would quickly recoup their outlay before the Public Health caught up with them. They bought, paying with suitcases full of cash. They rented off room by room as individual tenancies. No questions asked. No complaints listened to. No children permitted except on payment of extra rent. Some of the one-time mansions along Princes Avenue housed as many as 15 families at a time.

Thus I found myself the nominal representative of two entirely different sets of people: the established community with a firmly set way of life and the incomers whose only common bond was that they were rejected by the society in which they found themselves. At first only the longstanding residents came to our surgeries. I learned their story by heart and listened with compassion to their expressions of fear over the collapse of all that they held dear as their footholds were undermined and their way of life flouted. 'You didn't ever go up Berkley Street on a Sunday unless you had a white dress to wear... You always came up the back entry and in at the back door if you had your working clothes on...' A way of life vanished down the drain before my very eyes. Maybe it was no more than custom and habit, but it was the glue that had held them together as a community. Disintegration and fear set in, withdrawal behind a locked front door seemed to many the only refuge. Those that could, left. Many of the remainder pestered us as their Councillors to help them to get a transfer even if the only alternative was a tenancy in the outer Siberia of a housing estate. Shamefacedly, because they knew it was inadmissible, they admitted their main reason for wanting to leave was that 'the blacks have moved into our street'.

After a while and a deal of persuasion, I began to get the incomers too to come to my surgeries. I learned not to show surprise at some of the more eccentric domestic set-ups which I encountered. I learned true humility from the charity of the outcast for the outcast, and a deep respect for the true love and loyalty which many a couple displayed towards each other and to their children. I knew that I could not have coped with four young children in a tiny top floor room, sitting in Princes Park all day so that a husband on night-shift could get some sleep. I knew that I could not have shared a gas cooker on the landing with other women who burnt up my shillingsworth of gas when my back was turned. I could never have tolerated the solitary lavatory which had to serve the needs of a multi-occupied house, some of whose occupants had never been house-trained.

To be a City Councillor then was an unforgettable experience, torn as we were between the conflicting claims of the different sections among our constituents and swamped by a rising tide of need such as we had never before encountered, certainly not on such a scale or of such complexity. We struggled to offer whatever first aid we could without losing sight of the urgent need to attract attention to the fact that what we were undergoing was a crisis of a character quite new to our experience. The problems of the decay of the environment were commonplace all over the city and might have been stoically endured as such, but it was not the tangible grievances which brought a steady lengthening of the queues at our weekly surgeries till far into the night. Granby had been subjected to such an overloading of its capacity to cope with the social needs of those who lived there as to create a situation quite outside of our previous experience. The good and the bad, the rootless and the long-established, the victims of ill-fortune and those whose troubles were of their own making, any who by reason of the colour of their skin or some physical handicap were regarded as unacceptable, found themselves crammed together in one indistinguishable mass. The consequences were inevitable but all the harder to bear for that reason.

The unwritten rules and voluntary restrictions, the code of values, all the complex of convention and habit which hold a society together, proved to be totally inadequate to meet the needs of this melting pot of people. The well-established tradition of voluntary care by the community of any neighbour in distress and the spontaneous self-disciplining of any errant behaviour simply could not begin to meet the strain of the burden imposed on them. Many an individual struggled to do so but the sheer bulk of deprivation of every conceivable kind defeated their every endeavour.

In desperation we tried to attract attention to our plight. We had then no grasp of the fact that what we were witnessing was the onset of that collapse of our system of urban management which was to bring about the total breakdown of the riots of 20 years later. I recollect on one occasion making a speech to the City Council pleading for special discrimination in favour of Granby by saying that there was only one industry in the area, and that a singularly flourishing one, the production of social problems.

My fellow Councillors and I stood appalled on the sidelines watching as everything about us crumbled in slow motion. Unemployment rotted the foundations of family life. To be unwanted as workers when the docks closed and shipping diminished was the final injustice in a sequence of unmerited tribulation. Stress itself became a factor in causing stress.

Fragmentation bred fragmentation. Order collapsed into decay even as we watched.

Helpless in the face of such an irreversible downward spiral of disintegration, fear became almost as real a burden as any material deprivation, the panic fear of those trapped in a ghetto without hope or rescue and from which there is no escape. Fear turned to resentment as Rachmanism all too blatantly triumphed over those we had assumed to be in authority. 'Government' seemed as helpless as we were ourselves to reverse the desperation of our situation. 'We are forgotten people,' became the common cry at the plethora of residents' meetings at which we sought to convey our message to officials. Sheer frustration drove many into hostility towards all those in authority, not least the police. People in Granby knew by experience what I had learned from the teaching of Titmuss, that physical survival is not enough: to be deprived of the right to belong to a caring community is the ultimate deprivation. It was significant that when I protested that it was useless for people to come to see me so often since there was little that I could do, it was made perfectly clear that they were well aware of that fact: what was wanted of me was no more than that I should care.

The overloading of the public services throughout the 1960s, as the clearance of the University precinct peaked, brought about a full-scale crisis. Sheer pressure of numbers would have been enough in itself to breed aggression and violence but there was in addition the sporadic build-up of tensions between the established residents and the dispossessed incomers. As if that was not enough, a factor began to surface increasingly which was to prove to be as insidious and dangerous as dry rot in an old building, all the more so because it remained secret for so long. Liverpool's self-proclaimed freedom from racial prejudice was more and more clearly revealed as self-deception. What are now known as ethnic minorities had traditionally settled down by the riverside, near the south docks. This was generally assumed to be their proper place and they stayed in it. The blitz drove many inland to the slums round the University. The University clearance drove them on into Granby. Their numbers were increased by the arrival of West Indians, Africans, Chinese and Asians, though in comparatively small numbers, during and after the Second World War: Liverpool did not experience the postwar settlement of Commonwealth citizens found in more prosperous cities.

Like everyone else, this cosmopolitan group wanted only to establish decent lives for themselves and their families: the majority of the older generation, especially those from overseas, seemed prepared to pay almost any price to win acceptance and be left in peace. Their children, never having experienced the colonial tradition, tolerated no such inhibitions.

'Half-castes', as the children of mixed marriages were widely called, had not previously existed in sufficient numbers to attract attention as a community, but this no longer held good. A new generation had appeared on the scene. Liverpool born and bred, they took it for granted that they would be treated as such and were understandably resentful of their rejection by the community at large. Their case was a genuine one. When in 1968 the Youth Organisations Committee (a representative group concerned with youth work) prepared a commentary on the position of young 'coloured' people in the city, we deliberately chose as its title *Special But Not Separate*, to emphasise that though they might face special difficulties they were not for that reason to be set apart. It astonishes me now to see that though the report contained considerable evidence of racial prejudice, no mention was made of the police.

Recognition that inner city areas nationally called for urgent attention came with Harold Wilson's announcement in 1968 of the urban aid programme. Ominously, the spark which provoked Wilson's action was the public declaration by Enoch Powell of his forebodings on the theme of race. The shock and horror with which that speech was received locally was not so much for its content as because it brought out into the open something that till then had been secret and hidden. I still remember the curious mixture of furtive embarrassment and excitement with which people asked me the next day if I had heard...? Powell had pushed back the boundaries of decency in a way which rightly aroused revulsion and fear. 'We are creating a Harlem,' my husband warned in the House of Lords, 'we are creating a group of sub-standard citizens. That situation is about to become universal in this country. What now applies to Liverpool, and has obtained for 60 years in increasing degree, will shortly apply to all the big cities in England. And God help us if we lose equality of citizenship with people merely because they are coloured.' A ghetto was forming within the ghetto.

For my first few years as a Councillor, we were so engaged in the struggle to keep our heads above the foul waters of Rachmanism that we could pay little heed to anything other than survival. Where difficulty and distress were so universally distributed and the resources for their relief so thin upon the ground, it was all too easy to become bogged down under the overload of individual rescues. Yet, out of the sheer necessity of our situation came the promotion of a succession of schemes designed to restore to the local community something of the self-respect which had once characterised it. The story of those brave efforts and the part played in them by local people, both black and white, is one more example of Liverpool's talent for turning its liabilities to good use. The lessons to be learned merit more attention than is ever paid to them by those who in subsequent years have rushed to our assistance.

The lead came from the churches in the first instance. In flat contradiction of the sectarian traditions which have dominated Liverpool's history, all the local denominations came together to offer support to anybody and everybody who was prepared to fight back against the deprivations inflicted upon them. It was an astonishing experience, especially at that point in time, to attend a meeting of residents, initiated perhaps by the Methodists, chaired by an Anglican priest and held in Catholic premises. Under their joint auspices and with their most practical of assistance, the Granby Community Council came into being as a forum for the sharing of concern about local issues and a platform for effective protest. The purpose was to make it possible for individuals to have and to feel that they had some say in the management of their own affairs and to discover how best this could be done. A notable success was our opposition to the licensing of commercial night clubs which sought to use the existence of those maintained by groups from overseas for the benefit of their compatriots as grounds for obtaining planning permission for activities unwelcome to residents. I still relish the defeat of the great Mecca organisation who, as a guarantee of good behaviour, assured us and the Licensing Bench that they knew how to discriminate.

We fought the nuisance of kerb crawlers with ingenuity and zeal. Officials from departments such as housing, planning and lighting were persuaded to come before local gatherings to answer criticisms and explain their service programmes and policies. The managers of local schools were called together by the Chairman of Granby Street to form what proved to be a forerunner of the National Association of Governors and Managers, fondly known as NAG'M, pioneers of the campaign for recognition of the need for discrimination in favour of schools in areas of high priority.

More ambitiously, the Education Priority Area Campaign and the Shelter Neighbourhood Action Project (SNAP) demonstrated that, devised with ingenuity and presented with conviction, an alternative style of community management was a practical alternative. Both stood for a completely new orientation of policy so that management was based on the consent and with the advice of local people and was not imposed on them at the whim of those with power over them. 'Priority' dealt with the relationship between parents, schools and the local community, SNAP with the comprehensive programme for rehabilitation of all the services in 'the Granby triangle'. What fun we had. What dreams we dreamed. What first-rate work was done.

We were perhaps ahead of our time. Though participation was the flavour of the day, 'They' were not yet ready to go as far down the road as we demanded. Sundry pilot projects in the decentralisation of local authority administration found the going heavy and hard. Sadly, Shelter folded its tent and departed. As one of their reports put it, without a change of heart on the part of the establishment we could not hope to succeed and this they were not willing to accept. A similar fate for similar reasons befell Priority. It did not occur to us that what we were entering upon was the onset of what has come to be called 'the urban crisis' and to doubt that it might be beyond us locally to do anything more than cushion its effects on individuals. Much of what confronted us seemed to us be no more than the familiar cycle of urban deprivation, common to any inner area; unemployment, bad housing, inadequate education, wretched health. Clearance had not yet been started locally to any great extent, the fabric of social life though sadly torn was perhaps not beyond repair, and faith in reform by process of gradual change still held good.

Yet even while many of us toiled away at our endless meetings and working parties, a contrary tide of alienation from all that we stood for was sweeping beyond reach increasing numbers of the very people we sought to contact. For the situation was not static. Without conscious decision, Granby had come to be regarded as providing the answer to the perennial problem of every big city. What to do with 'the poor or the black'? One of our young planners argued that the City Council should openly designate an area specifically for their reception. Every city needs a dustbin, he assured me. It became an accepted fact of life to housing officials, welfare workers and the police that Granby was a problem area and therefore fit accommodation for those who in themselves constituted a 'problem' for the city. As official practices worked out on the ground, many of the younger and more effective moved away, while opportunities of escape for those who remained became increasingly difficult. Merely to live in Granby was a handicap to anyone in search of a job, an insurance policy or even a booking in a holiday camp.

A creeping sense of rejection was shared by all: the scale of it was a new phenomenon in my experience. Anxiety hardened into the conviction that 'They', whoever they were, had forgotten our existence. 'They' did what they thought was good for us regardless of our real and desperate needs. 'They' regarded us with contempt. 'They' never listened to what we had to say. Increasingly it seemed as if even the police were on 'Their' side, that they too regarded Granby as a problem community, outside the pale of decent society. Against this forced alienation, our talk of shared responsibility faltered and flagged. Hopelessness and helplessness chased each other in a downward spiral of despair.

The common reaction was one of withdrawal which was mistaken for apathy. Only those who remembered another way of life were interested in my talk about 'the community': they still cherished a vision even if it consisted of nostalgia for the past rather than hope for a brave new future.

Increasingly, they found themselves to be in the minority, their dwindling numbers off-set by the multiplication of those who had no share in that memory of the past and saw in it no hope of a better future. A plague of amateur anarchists descended upon us, long-haired young men who affected dirty white plimsolls and found the weekly dole quite adequate to their way of life. They preached a gospel of voluntary exclusion which fitted precisely the mood of the young and the disaffected. It was but a short step from resentment to hostility and eventually retaliation. Trouble on the streets became a commonplace for many people. A voluntary curfew after the hours of darkness became a habit of living. Our surgeries were changed from week-nights to Saturday mornings.

Yet out of that universal sense of rejection and alienation a curious cohesion of despair began to develop for the first time I had ever known in that polyglot community. When my husband was made a life peer in order that he might go to the aid of the party in the Lords, it was in tribute to that growing solidarity that he chose to be known as Simey of Toxteth. To claim Liverpool 8 as your address became a sort of snobbery to those of us who lived there; we took a kind of inverted pride in coming at the top of the list in any catalogue of deprivation.

It was only a matter of time before what had come about was to be given official confirmation. After the 1981 disturbances, a scheme for intensive beat policing was instituted for the area which had experienced the brunt of the disorder. It was no cause for surprise that there for all to see on the walls of the Hope Street police station hung the map of what had become the ghetto.

2

The Building of a Bonfire

I was under no delusions as to what I could hope to achieve when I set out on my career as a City Councillor in 1963. Sitting on the edge of my bed late on the night of Election day, too tired even to undress, there was no vestige of the usual elation of victory. 'What have we let ourselves in for?', I asked my husband, eyeing with foreboding the tangle of problems which demanded solution. It certainly never dawned on me that the future would see the focus of my attention narrow increasingly upon the police to the point at which there would be little room for anything else. Or that policing would emerge as the prime illustration of the disastrous consequences of the separation of government from the governed.

It is only with hindsight that I realise the significance of the fact that I can now recollect only one incident in my first campaign in Granby. This was a street corner encounter with a scrap metal merchant, though that is a rather grand description of his hand-to-mouth struggle for survival. He listened to my ladylike little spiel about being the Labour candidate and then he said, 'What are you going to do about the police?' I fumbled it: the police have a difficult job to do, and so on, but I really had no clue as to what he was on about. So far as we as Councillors were concerned, the relationship with the police was merely one amongst the many problems to come our way. Punch drunk, we reeled from one crisis to another as education, unemployment, and always, always, housing screamed at us for action. We spared time to protest against the amalgamation of the Liverpool and Bootle Forces into one because of the consequent lack of direct accountability by them to either of the Councils but that apart, policing merited no special priority. The situation was, however, far from static — as we were to discover.

What befell Granby during the 1960s provides a classic illustration of the consequences of the breakdown of what might be called the community's 'standing orders', the arrangements, both formal and informal, for managing its common affairs. These proved to be hopelessly inadequate to the demands of what by the end of the decade had become a crisis. This was peculiarly evident so far as the relations between the generations were concerned. Driven on to the streets by the overcrowding in their homes, increasingly without employment as the decline of the port accelerated, young people looked about them for alternative occupation. Inevitably, trouble ensued either amongst themselves or with the adult community. Frequently, and on occasion regardless of the colour of their skin, they closed ranks against their elders. At other times, black lads felt as if they were under siege by white gangs from outside the area. In that disintegrated society, defiance of authority in whatever shape or form could with impunity be taken to hitherto unheard of extremes. The generation gap assumed alarming proportions.

To a public verging on panic, the police provided the obvious solution. Only the police had the power to compel the obedience of unruly youngsters. They were the last visible symbols of that safety and security which were so notably absent from daily life. This put the police in a quandary. Accustomed as they were to policing the Granby area in the traditional father-figure style they found themselves swamped by the welter of problems which were now off-loaded on to them. With genuine concern for the people who turned to them but without thought for the consequences, they allowed themselves to be pushed into a role which was curiously parallel to that of the Relieving Officer of old. They were pressed to join the committees of youth clubs, to assist with pensioners' dinner clubs, to attend case conferences about children in danger, resolve domestic disputes, restore peace between uncongenial neighbours; all these as well as call the attention of 'the Corpy' to the need for repairs to pavements, streetlights and leaking roofs. I protested that if they continued to add to their responsibilities in this way they would find themselves emptying the dustbins as well. 'Our shoulders are broad,' was their proud reply.

Unhappily, in that volatile and overcrowded setting, there was little vestige of the stable society which was the usual framework for traditional British policing. Shocked by the mounting disorder of a severely disrupted society, the Force came to assume that the whole community was a hotch-potch of criminality, guilty until they proved their innocence. By tradition, they relied on force rather than persuasion (the first time I ever heard the phrase 'physical policing' was in Liverpool) but the more vigorously they tried to exercise their authority, the more openly hostile their reception. A certain animosity to those in authority is a commonplace of inner city life but the hostility which the police now began to encounter was something they had never experienced before.

Being literally all too obvious, the 'half-castes' became the scapegoats whenever trouble broke. To be young, male and particularly to be a locally-born Black became a recipe for automatic suspicion. That this identification by the police of skin colour with disorder might be interpreted as racism was hotly denied. Antagonism to the use of the power to stop and search people in the street became the focus of mounting protest about policing practice even amongst the adult community; this was nothing like the policing of their dreams. Mutual recrimination became the habit of the day. Swamped as we Councillors were by complaints of rough handling and racial abuse on the part of the police, it was increasingly difficult to determine where the truth lay. My inbred 'liberalism' was strained to its limits. Perversely the cry went up for more power to the elbow of the Force, more money, more everything they asked for.

All this was deeply disturbing but my thoughts still turned more to the prevention of trouble than to questioning police tactics. I was proud of the fact that 'The Methodist' had earned for itself the reputation of being the one youth club where young and adolescent people could feel secure from threat; there seemed no way in which we could usefully get to grips with the fact that the 'threat' from which they sought protection came from the police. To do them justice, there were amongst the police those who realised the urgency of the situation which was developing and the setting up of a scheme to foster relationships with the Black community was a pioneering effort. Individual officers began to make contact with local people, the Deputy Chief Constable, for example, making a habit of dropping in for a drink at the bar of the local 'Community Centre for Coloured People and Their Friends'.

Then came the case of Lenny Cruikshank. Lenny was a locally-born young Black whom I knew because he was a street representative at residents' meetings of the Shelter project known as SNAP. He worked as a gardener in the Parks and Gardens Department. Outside the project hut one dark evening in 1970, he buttonholed me. He was in trouble with the police and it wasn't true and would I be a character witness for him. I hesitated because I only knew him rather casually but I took my obligations as a Councillor seriously so I agreed. Lenny had been going home late at night from a folk club event in a pub with a guitar under his arm. Police in a jeep stopped him: two am by the Rialto Cinema, a young Black man carrying a bulky object; surely it was 'reasonable' to stop and question him? But our Lenny was a Scouser by birth and upbringing and though I daresay he answered correctly enough, the police took exception to his manner. He ended up in temporary detention at the Dale Street Bridewell, where, he claimed, he had been thumped and abused. And, in addition, he was charged with possession of a small twist of cannabis. Lenny swore it had been planted on him by the police.

It is indicative of the isolation of the police from mainstream politics that it never occurred to me to enlist the help of anyone either in the Force or on the Police Committee. I had already tried going to see the police on other occasions but each time they had patted me on the head, said that it wasn't right for a nice lady like me to be mixed up in such goings-on and just to run away and leave it all to them. I could have asked questions at the City Council but the Police Committee was a strangely autonomous and elusive body, very much the private preserve of the Alderman who chaired it.

Some hunch inspired me to go down to St George's Hall the day the trial began. I was depressed to find that Lenny's legal representative perked up no end when he found that 'Lady Simey' was interested; till then it had obviously been a routine 'sus' case to him. Lenny insisted that there were eight officers at various times in the Bridewell, and that one of them wore a canary-yellow pullover. Six officers gave evidence. Six swore that only they had been present. None had worn a yellow jersey. I began to lose confidence. After all, what did I know of Lenny? The human race is always fallible. That took us from a Thursday through to about the following Wednesday. Then justice was unexpectedly done. Passing across the main arena of St George's Hall, a vast Victorian space crowded with men in wig and gown, and huddles of people being shepherded in to act as juries, Lenny spied the two missing men. Melodrama! Subpoenas issued there and then. Two further officers to give evidence. Yes, they had been there. Yes, one of them had a yellow jersey: he was actually wearing it which was how Lenny spotted him. The jury took 15 minutes. Case dismissed.

I kissed Lenny, embraced his sundry relatives, and walked out into Lime Street, feeling that the foundations of civilisation were rocking beneath my feet. That the police should lie; that the police *could* lie. All the endless incidents that had been reported to me which I had found it impossible to believe, the outcries in Court about police abuse when I was sitting as a magistrate, surfaced in my mind. Naively I assumed that the entire Force must be shuddering from the shock and shame of it. I couldn't bring myself to mention it to them, so full of pity was I for the hurt they must be suffering. Innocent fool! It was quite some time before I dared raise the matter with them, only to learn that only an internal inquiry had been held because there had been no formal complaint, which it had never occurred to me to make.

Doubts, once sown, sprouted like weeds. There were too many complaints for them all to be lies. I became involved in various 'watchdog' schemes, one of which ended particularly disastrously when an over-zealous member fabricated a series of juicy incidents by way of supporting his assertions of police ill-treatment. BBC Radio Merseyside decided to do a programme on allegations of police brutality. They sniffed out a variety of evidence. A number of us were interviewed: a Councillor colleague who, as a doctor, could speak of cases of alleged police violence amongst his patients; me, of course; and as the star witness, a young policewoman who told of hearing officers talk of 'going farming' and 'agriculture' as terms for sweeps in the Granby area perhaps involving drug planting against the Blacks. I realise now how very damning her evidence was. Her identity was soon discovered and she was interrogated. She vanished on sick leave. The impression we got was that those in authority were far more concerned with disciplining her than with tackling the allegations which had been made.

The police then set about trying to work up a case against the staff of Radio Merseyside for suborning the loyalty of the woman police officer. They involved me because I was said to have offered her an inducement by guaranteeing her a job as a school welfare officer, if she was dismissed from the Force. The head of the murder squad and a companion were sent to interview me at home. It ended up with the pair of them defending themselves against my accusation that the police provoked violence in Granby by the tactics they adopted, and were themselves responsible for the intensity of the anti-police reaction. It became not a little farcical when this very senior officer pleaded with me rather pathetically to tell him: 'Why don't people like us?'

All this attracted massive publicity. My 'phone rang right round the clock. I was so scandalised by the stand taken by the police that I was easy game for publicity-seeking journalists. All the more so because by now tension in the ward was such that I accepted, as did many others, that trouble was just round the corner. The Falkner Estate riots of 1972, though they bear no comparison with more recent events, were evidence of serious unrest. For me, personally, there was trouble too from the leader of the Council who feared that my forecast of civil war in the streets of Granby would earn the Labour Party the reputation of being anti-police. My ward colleagues stood by me, however, as did local workers such as probation officers, who felt that by exposing the situation the tension had at least been temporarily released. My outbursts evidently put into words what a lot of people had felt but dared not cry out loud, or if they did so, they went unheard. Hence my sudden acquisition of fame as a woman of courage. If I was courageous it was not because I acted on principle but that having said my piece publicly, I lacked the nerve to be seen to run away from the stand I had taken.

It might have been expected that a change would come over the scene with the setting up of the Metropolitan County Councils in 1974 and the consequent appointment by each of them of a properly constituted subcommittee to act as Police Authority. On Merseyside, Labour won the elections. I was once more elected for Granby and, to my surprise, found myself appointed Deputy Chairman of the new committee. When the whips sent round their usual chit, I had not even put down Police as a committee on which I should like to serve. This was cowardice, though I told myself that it would be a waste of time to try because no one in their senses would select me: a woman, with a considerable record of police-knocking, representative of the so-called criminal community, already an OAP. In those days the leader of the party dispensed office in Chicago-boss style; I was told years later that I was appointed to keep me out of mischief.

Though it was some time before we realised it, the Police Authority was a very strange beast indeed and one whose nature was a constitutional curiosity not easily to be comprehended. It owed its existence to the fact that the County Council was required by law to set up a committee to act as a Police Authority. No one at that stage questioned the assumption that this should be the Committee's sole function. Nor was there any apprehension as to the peculiar anomaly that while as the Police Committee we were presumably accountable to the County Council, as the Police Authority we were largely autonomous. Decisions which involved expenditure had to be submitted to the County Council for approval though no one asked what would happen if this was refused. As to what our powers and duties might be, no one seemed to have any idea except that they were singularly ill-defined and appeared to overlap if not duplicate those of our chief officer. When we were firmly told by so important a personage as the Chief Constable that a matter was 'operational' and therefore beyond our jurisdiction, who were we to argue? Our moment of greatest glory came when senior appointments were to be made. I recollect the sense of gratification with which we appointed Mr Oxford, first as our Deputy and then in 1976 as our Chief Constable. His enthusiasm for the vital contribution to be made by elected members warmed our hearts and fed our vanity. And of course we enjoyed the Annual Horse Show with its lunch of fresh salmon and strawberries and cream, while the police band played outside under the trees. I only discovered how forbiddingly large a police horse can be when I reached up to fasten a rosette on the bridle of a winner.

At a loss for any better idea, we busied ourselves with the manifold details of bringing into existence the brand new Merseyside Police Force. This was impressively large, judging by previous standards, being composed of the Liverpool and Bootle Force plus others from Lancashire and Cheshire, bits of whose territory constituted the new County of Merseyside. The welding together into a single unit of these often un-willing recruits to our service was a tricky business which we were happy to accept was 'operational' and therefore not our responsibility. On the other hand, the preparation and implementation of a comprehensive building programme to replace the outworn local stations we had inherited and to provide a headquarters worthy of the enlarged Force was a procedure with which many of us were familiar. (Gossip had it that the Lancashire and Cheshire Forces had reorganised their entire stock so that all the chairs without legs and the typewriters beyond redemption were passed to us. The same was said of the manpower.) Going on tour to 'see for ourselves' kept us harmlessly and happily occupied for years.

This was all very well and really rather enjoyable so far as it went but it did absolutely nothing to answer the growing volume of protest about police behaviour in the inner areas of which I as a local Councillor was acutely aware. Desperate to do something to relieve my feelings of frustration, I rashly set out to institute an Advisory Committee that would compensate for the lack of inner area experience on the part of most members of the Authority. It was a lost cause if ever there was one. Subtly I was made to realise that the Authority itself was only an advisory body and not an executive committee which was a polite way of saying that we were a rubber stamp. I cannot now remember how it was wrapped up or what face-saving device was used, but the project quietly faded from sight. I got the impression that the Police Federation disapproved and that that was decisive. It was my first encounter with the capacity of the Force to close ranks.

Gradually it began to dawn on me that though by law we were responsible for providing an adequate and efficient Force, we seemed to have no power to do anything to bring this about. Responsibility and power had parted company in some mysterious fashion. It took us the best part of our first term in office to comprehend the baffling fact that as a committee we were unable to make any kind of effective intervention in the administration of the service of which we had supposed ourselves to be in control. Those who have never themselves experienced the reality of trying to put the 1964 Police Act into practice are free in their criticism that Police Authorities are lax in the exercise of their powers and duties. This is totally to fail to appreciate the subtleties of the situation. We ourselves only came to grips with it not so much by trial and error as by what felt like blundering into obstacles in a thick fog on a dark night.

Certainly the legislation was woolly in the extreme but gradually we realised that there was more to our problem than that. With growing incredulity we began to sense that policing was a sacred cow of huge and totally unsuspected dimensions. It was taboo even to ask for information as to the nature of the beast, let alone what purpose it served or who was in charge of it. I remember being sharply urged by my own colleagues to behave myself because of the damage my enthusiasm for asking awkward questions was doing to the image of the party. No matter what was going on in Granby, no way was it permissible to utter any word that seemed to imply criticism of the British bobby.

The power of that intangible taboo, supported as it was with emotion and vehemence by police and public alike, is hard to convey, all the more so because it is now so freely challenged. Courage and conviction were needed to stand up against it. Courage we could scrape together but confidence was harder to come by. If we were not already aware of our inadequacies, the Chief Constable's recurrent public denunciation of politicians as being ignorant and ill-informed rubbed the lesson home. Yet our earnest endeavours to remedy our ignorance were blocked by the ban on any attempt on our part to improve our knowledge of what was regarded as operational. We were not even sure what questions we ought to ask. Thus we were trapped in a vicious circle whose grip was tightened by the Force's arrogant assertion of autonomy.

Meanwhile, the situation in Granby was fast developing into a demonstration of the futility of meeting violence with violence. There could be no question of attributing blame for this; the pattern of tit-for-tat stretched too far into Liverpool's past for that kind of exercise to be of any value. The Force backed the Chief in declaring that our troubles stemmed from the presence in our midst of the 'coloured', stoutly denying that this stood for prejudice. The Black community strongly resented the fundamental injustice of such a condemnation.

What provoked a particularly angry reaction was the belief that the police were abusing their special powers under a local bye-law to stop and search anyone who could reasonably be suspected of having stolen goods in their possession. They had originally secured these powers to deal with stealing on the docks but it was commonly felt that they were being used as an instrument of social control in a way which had never been intended and which was bitterly resented. A typical tale of the times had it that a Black lad, returning from the laundrette with his mother's washing, was stopped by a policeman who enquired what was in the bag and to whom it belonged. The boy answered, adding that he lived just across the street and the officer was welcome to call and verify his story. Instead he was taken to the police station where, because of the vigour of his protest when stopped, he was charged with obstruction. His mother's arrival established the ownership of the washing all right but she expressed her indignation even more forcibly and was charged with disorderly behaviour. Both appeared in Court, were duly fined, and placed on the records as 'criminals'. Neither charge related to the original reason for stopping the lad.

It was hard, on first hearing, to take this seriously. Surely this was ludicrous: no such thing could possibly happen. And if indeed it did, then it must have been a one-off, an excess of zeal on the part of some young constable new to the job. Yet variations on this theme recurred so often, particularly but by no means solely in the inner city, that it earned the label of the Bagwash Syndrome. Little groups such as Mums Against Sus arose spontaneously out of the need for self-defence.

Ironically, it was only after the Tories took charge in May 1977 that the issue of the Police Authority's role developed a sufficient head of steam for the situation on the Committee to blow. I became opposition spokesman, leader of a noble band of five, one of whom was a sick man and two with other interests. Luckily for me, my second man was a Councillor of vast experience as a member for Knowsley, which comprised Kirkby and Huyton. We had to step very gingerly at committees because, there being so few of us, we inevitably appeared to hog the debate. The Tories would groan out loud if I spoke too often, with cries of 'She's off again . . . move next business'. Not pleasant or easy, especially for a middle-class woman who had been reared to please.

Then came the Kelly case. Jimmy Kelly was an unemployed labourer, living in Huyton. One summer evening in 1979, he was making his way home across a vacant site after a night out, singing happily enough. A police van arrived, scooped him up with some little difficulty, and drove him off to the police station. Various people watched from nearby flats and subsequently gave differing accounts. All very typical of life in Huyton, except for the fact that Kelly was dead by midnight.

This was the last in a series of incidents involving allegations of police brutality in the Knowsley Division, and a right public fuss broke out. The previous cases of Blair Peach in London, and Liddell Towers on Tyneside ensured that we got full media attention. In true Scouse style, a committee of local people was smartly formed, collections made in pubs, and protest marches organised. The furore drove the Chief Constable to invite an officer from another Force to investigate. Enter one of the chief characters in the drama: Mr Gerty from the West Midlands Force. The air was thick with rumour and gossip; Mr Gerty was an old Met buddy of the Chief; Mr Gerty was only checking over the reports already assembled by the local Force; Mr Gerty was doing this, that and the other, all of it suspect. Trying to be helpful (though in subsequent years I have been credited with making a calculated master stroke) I put the simplest of questions to the Chief at the next committee, well aware that I must be careful not to provoke the reply that the case was sub judice. 'Would the Chief tell us,' I asked in my best ladylike voice, 'is Mr Gerty here to investigate just the Kelly case or all the seventeen other complaints in Knowsley?' 'No,' he replied, 'I won't.' And added for good measure that we could look to the local press if we wanted any further information.

Talk about balloons going up! Some of the committee had found it possible to disbelieve the stories by people who lived in Granby especially if those involved were Black, but this was something quite different. Never mind the pros and cons of how a man had been treated, what mattered to us was how we elected members had been treated. All three parties were united in furious resentment of such behaviour by a chief officer, even if he was the Chief Constable. We learned more in the next few weeks about the restrictions on our capacity as elected members than we had managed to do in all the six previous years. The status of the Clerk, who happened to be the County Solicitor; the power of the Chief; the dismal uncertainty of our own role, if any: all became topics of the day. A major debate in the County Council ranged far and wide and thoughts were given open expression which previously had only been murmured behind closed doors. The Conservative Chairman of the County Council wrote a letter to *The Times* (May 1980) calling attention to the unacceptable arrogance of Chief Constables in general and ours in particular.

At our request, the County Solicitor prepared a report on 'The Role and Responsibility of a Police Authority' which, so it was said, was from then on to be found on the desk of every Chief in the country. This was the first of a series of reports of which the Authority was justly proud but though it spelled out all the relevant legislation for the first time, which was useful, this merely highlighted the ambiguities embodied in the 1964 Act and did nothing to resolve them. As far as we could see, Committee and chief officer had identical briefs.

This state of guerrilla warfare spluttered on between us for some time. But not for long. Fresh trouble broke out and this time, because it concerned the spending of public money, there could be no doubt that politicians must be allowed to bear at least some share of the responsibility. The 'Great Budget Row' which ensued put solid ground under our feet at last. This time the cause of the trouble lay in the fact that till 1980, the Force had never before managed to recruit up to its full establishment, and since the government grant is based on the paper figure and not the actual manpower, there had always been enough financial 'slack' to keep everyone happy. Rising unemployment upset that applecart by improving recruitment. Simultaneously, the police were at long last required to accept some share in the government's drive for cuts in the public services. The Conservative majority on our Police

Authority had no option but to comply, imposing a cut on overtime of several millions. Predictably, the police were aghast. Never before had their expenditure been subjected to such action; they assumed that as by divine right they had merely to ask in order to receive all that they thought necessary.

Come January 1981, the Authority met to consider its budget in the lecture hall of the County Museum, a slightly sinister rectangle of a room without windows. As we filed in from our respective group meetings, we were amazed to find it packed to capacity with a mass of senior officers, a number in uniform. We felt intimidated, though the Chief later made it known that his intention was only to let his officers see what he had to put up with. There was a TV team at the doors and reporters galore within. As was customary the Chief was invited to lead off. This he did in a long, prepared speech, denunciatory in tone, and containing phrases like 'teeming and lading' referring to the Treasurer and 'piracy' with reference to the members. Reluctantly he indicated that he would nevertheless accept a reduction of the amount allocated to overtime.

The Tory Chairman was visibly shaken. After his long track record of unstinting loyalty to the Force, to be publicly denounced for his failure to give support was so unjust as to reduce him near to tears. Shocked to the core, he briefly moved acceptance of the budget, complete with cuts. What the Chief expected to happen next, goodness knows, but it cannot have been what actually occurred. Making no comment, I formally seconded the resolution. Without debate, we approved the entire budget in one full swoop and all was over. There were plenty of questions which could have been asked, and normally should have been, but for sheer political impact, it could not have been bettered. It was a spontaneous declaration of solid opposition to the assumption of autonomy by the Chief, which almost constituted a vote of no confidence.

Consternation broke out on all fronts. Secret all-party meetings were held to discuss strategy in so unusual a situation. Gossip has it that when the Tory spokesmen went by air to call upon the Home Secretary for support, they were embarrassed to find the Chief Constable aboard the same 'plane, presumably on the same errand. The situation was unprecedented. After much parleying, the Home Secretary proving unresponsive, a face-saving operation was mounted which resulted in agreement that there should be closer consultation in future. This left the issue unresolved. Did the Chief's autonomy cover the spending of cash for which we were accountable, possibly on policies of which we might not approve? Were we there merely to pay up and shut up? There could hardly be hope of providing an efficient and effective service while questions of this magnitude remained to haunt us.

For me, the gulf between the reality of the growing tension in Granby and the frustration of any and every attempt to have it discussed at Committee became ever harder to bear. It strained belief that the kindly father figures so stoutly defended by the Chief could be one and the same as the bullies whose treatment of local lads was said to amount to open oppression. There seemed to be two faces to policing, one for the 'goodies' and the very different face presented to those whom the police and many of the public labelled as 'baddies'. I began to receive outraged accounts from those in the first category who had inadvertently strayed into the second, as in the case of the young clergyman in his off-duty jeans who encountered the rough tongue of the law when questioned as to the ownership of the car he was driving. We struggled to use the complaints system but eventually came to the conclusion that it was geared solely to questions of in-force discipline and was irrelevant to expressions of dissatisfaction by the public as consumers. The unquestioning loyalty of the Force to their own members undermined whatever confidence might have been placed in official investigations.

With incredulity I found myself forced to admit that racism seemed to be inherent in the relationship between police and the Black community. The law must pay no attention to the colour of a man's skin, we were roundly assured; yet justice required that neither should those who enforced it and this was manifestly not so. Time and again some hapless bobby betrayed the assumption that to be Black was reasonable ground for suspicion. A case which gave rise to much ironic hilarity was that of a Black police sports coach who suffered acute indignity on being 'sussed' by reason of the colour of his skin.

The tension of the troubled relationship between police and policed in the inner area moved inexorably towards breaking point. 'Black violence simmers in unemployment-hit Liverpool' was typical headline stuff. My bitter prophecy that there would be civil war in the streets of Granby unless something was done to end gang warfare between young policemen and the young of Liverpool 8 was reiterated by the highly-respected Chairman of the Afro-Asian Standing Committee. 'Someone is going to say, to hell with it,' he warned, 'to hell with it; let's burn the place down.' Already the debate was on as to whether the appropriate police response should be the aggressive tactics of an army of occupation. Riot gear in the shape of plastic shields had already been used by police in responding to an incident some years earlier, much to the astonishment of the locals. The Chief gave the public the most vigorous assurances that he was not prepared to tolerate mindless hooliganism and would take appropriate action to put a stop to it, whatever that might mean.

This then was my inheritance when, in May 1981, Labour won the elections and I found myself selected Chairman of the Police Authority. I was more surprised than elated, and eyed the future with apprehension and misgiving. On the one hand was a situation of public unrest and hostility so acute as to show every sign of developing into a major breakdown of law and order. On the other, between the Authority and the Chief, there was a division of opinion as to the allocation of responsibility so profound as to undermine the whole structure. Undoubtedly, a bonfire was a-building which it might well be beyond our capacity to extinguish.

3

The Road to Damascus

Labour won the County Council elections in May 1981. The initial meeting of the Authority took place in June. On the first weekend of July, the riots began. This came as no surprise to those familiar with the neighbourhood, though the Chief declared them to be unpredictable and unforeseen. Locally we had for some time ceased to talk in terms of 'if' there would be riots but simply of 'when'. There had been a successive closure by the police of the only downtown clubs where teenagers were tolerated. No doubt they were pretty grotty, drugs were peddled, and all manner of 'undesirables' gathered there but at least, in the classic phrase, they kept the young off the streets. With the closure of the last of them, Granby had become noticeably more noisy, more tense, especially on Fridays, the traditional occasion for a night out. Young people just stood about. The police moved them on. Verbal exchanges took place, usually of a mutually offensive nature. It filled in the time. We held our breath.

Hope rose for a brief moment when, in a remarkable demonstration of co-operation between police and community, trouble was averted on the occasion of an unwelcome intrusion into Granby by the National Front. The expression of resentment on the part of local people had brought out the police in a disturbing show of force but the personal intervention, literally on the street, of the Deputy Chief Constable and an outstanding Black community worker led to the withdrawal of both sides from the scene of the trouble.

Then on Friday, 4 July, a lad on a motorcycle was stopped by the police who questioned his ownership of it. A crowd of youths joined in. The lad escaped with their assistance, but a bystander was arrested. There were protests that the police only picked on him because they already knew him and his family. Confusion ensued. Shouting. Trouble. All the next day, Saturday, there was telephoning and anxiety. As the evening wore on, it was clear that real trouble was brewing. At midnight I was wakened by someone ringing at the front door. I put my head out of the window. There on the doorstep was a locally-born young Black community worker. I took him up to my kitchen. He was shivering with shock, not fear. There was violence at the top of Upper Parliament Street. Relations with the police had broken down. He and the handful of others like him could do no more. The fragile liaison with the Deputy Chief which had shown such promise only a couple of weeks before could do nothing against the ferocious hostility which had broken loose. Off he went into the night. It was useless for me, an old woman, to follow him; he assured me that I would only be in the way. The crowd was out of control.

On Sunday the situation exploded. That night was 'cops and robbers' stuff, literally run riot. All and sundry leapt on the bandwagon. Violence. Looting. Vandalism. Protest. The settling of old scores. A witches' brew which ended up with Lodge Lane in flames, the Social Services Office, the Rialto Cinema and the gentlemen's Racquets Club all burnt out. The hospital for old women was evacuated, Black and white alike helping patients to safety. The police applied only their traditional technique of linking arms to hold back the crowd. Slowly they retreated before the onslaught of violence. An extraordinary air of carnival developed, but carnival degenerate, vicious. The Vandals had indeed come to town.

Later, I was told in confidence, because the convention of loyalty to their own kind against authority still held good and runs very deep, of the shock of neighbour recognising neighbour merrily looting the shops in Lodge Lane. The police commented that though the rioting was mainly attributable to the locals, both white and Black, the looting was largely done by white adults, many from outside the area. There were authenticated stories of friends in the outer suburbs being rung up to come quickly while the going was good. People were observed ferrying goods in supermarket trolleys to unload into the boot of their cars, just as if they were on an ordinary shopping expedition. The next morning, trolleys were to be seen abandoned in back entries and on waste ground for miles around. The looting took on all the fun of the January Sales, and roused the same ugly competitiveness and the same excitement of grabbing something for nothing.

I sat on my bed watching the flames and smoke shoot up beyond the roofs of the houses in the next street. People rang me. As if I could intervene. The Senior Officer of the Community Relations Council arrived to report with incredulity that the police were retreating down Upper Parliament Street towards the City Centre. There was fear in the air. I began to collect some clothing and some money and, for some strange reason, my passport. Then abruptly, the flames died down and the shouting died away. Though I didn't know it, the police had used CS gas for the first time in mainland Britain. Some said the orgy was already past its peak, and that anyhow the crowds would never have moved outside their own familiar territory. Hundreds of officers were injured.

My recollection of the days and nights that followed is one of my utter helplessness. This was it, what we had been waiting for. As a Councillor for the area, as Chairman of the Police Authority no less, what should I do? I went out to see for myself. Before I even reached Upper Parliament Street, a car whizzed up, two men from CID bundled me into it, and smartly deposited me on my own doorstep before I could begin to argue. Ignominious, and a clear indication of what they thought of me and my role.

What should I do? The County officials were hard at it with the emergency services, getting street lights restored, clearing up the broken glass, pulling down unsafe buildings, doing all they could to aid the victims whose lives and property were wrecked. The police faced a breakdown of law and order such as none of us had previously encountered. The nights which lay ahead must surely bring further outbreaks of disorder. Over us all hung the fear of yet more violence, injury and perhaps death.

Never had I been more acutely conscious of the logic of the argument that it was not our job as elected representatives to meddle in things 'operational'. If ever there was a situation that could be so classified, this was surely it. There could be no room for us in such a crisis situation. Or could there? No one seemed even to know of our existence. No one cared a dump about the Chairman of the Police Authority. Desperately I tried to work out what, if anything, I ought to do. It seems extraordinary now to recollect that no one from the media thought of contacting me in my official capacity. Nevertheless there could be no escaping the fact that policing was increasingly seen to be at the heart of the matter, so we had surely some responsibility. On the one hand there was an angry and frightened public ready to condemn Blacks, rioters, looters in one indiscriminate lump and eager to rush to the support of the police in their efforts to restore order regardless of how they did it. On the other hand there was anxious concern that the use of CS gas had far-reaching implications. There was, too, troubled speculation that the immediate if not the long-term cause of the outbreak could be attributed to the overreaction of the police to a minor incident and their application of an aggressive style of policing to what was effectively a ghetto of deprivation. The Police Federation was vociferous. Their indignation was countered by that of the L8 Defence Committee, self-appointed spokesmen for the area, to the annoyance of the local 'respectables' but the delight of the media: they were highly articulate, handsome, and photogenic. Emotion began to pile up behind a campaign for the removal of the Chief Constable.

As the argument blazed into a fury of allegation and counter-allegation, I became increasingly confident that here lay our responsibility. What was at issue was emphatically not something that could be withdrawn from public scrutiny as 'operational' but was essentially and inescapably political, calling for political discussion and political decision. This conviction on my part strengthened as the local campaign against the Chief Constable in person gathered force. 'Oxford Must Go' was shouted in the streets. 'Oxford Out' was daubed on the walls. In these circumstances surely the last person to determine the outcome should be the individual concerned. Responsibility must rest squarely with the elected members charged by law with providing a service acceptable to the people. How to handle so highly-charged a situation remained as forbidding a task as ever but at least I was much clearer in my own mind as to what part my committee and I had to play.

It was this new sense of confidence on my part, even though I doubt if it was one shared by many others at that stage, which helped me to live through the weeks that followed. How to put my 'convictions' into practice, given the intensity of the anti-police lobby on the one hand and the intransigence of the Force in their response to it on the other. Whose side was I on, demanded the Federation. I wondered, myself. As a committee, we had to assert our existence. The necessity to take practical decisions forced the issue. It might be for the Chief to state his requirements but it was for us to authorise the spending of money, for instance on the purchase of riot gear. A good deal of mental anguish went into balancing the pros and cons of the possible use of plastic bullets in the future with all its practical connotations before we could decide just how we ought to handle such a debatable issue. We had no doubt, however, that the handling of the anti-Oxford campaign and the urgent need for an impartial assessment of policing politics, both during the riots and more generally, were matters for the Authority.

By this time the media were all over the place. Apart from the Kelly case and the 'Great Budget Row', they had ignored our existence for years. Now they began to pack the public gallery at every meeting. I fenced verbally, desperate to cool our performance. I walked a tight-rope. At our caucus meetings, I was under attack for being mealy-mouthed and pro-police. There were strained special meetings of the Authority where I tried to express concern for the ordeal the police had endured, especially the hundreds of wounded and those in hospital, conscious all the time of the glowering disapproval of my more militant members. They wanted me to condemn the police outright and I, being double their age and far more experienced, thought it was too early for condemnation and that whether the police were badly led or not, many had done their duty with courage and loyalty. Whatever was best to do? I longed to say to the police that I had told them so, years ago; that they should have listened then. My heart was deeply committed to the Blacks who had suffered injustice for years untold. And yet my instinct was all for restoring calm, for mediation instead of confrontation. Was that weakness or strength? Should I have defied the great mass of the public who were startled and afraid and needed reassurance? No wonder politicians get the reputation of being mealy-mouthed and evasive.

I cannot now remember what it was that triggered off the second outbreak of rioting three weeks later. That weekend the ward had decided to distribute a leaflet. I forget what it was about but I thought it irrelevant and a waste of time. However, I undertook to do the area that was called the 'Black Square' because I was the only member who showed a special interest in that particular section. It lay behind the recently burnt-out ruins of the Rialto block. I duly set off on the Saturday, and again the Sunday, early in the morning before people were up because I wanted to avoid getting involved in argument. I was tired and overstrained before I even started. It was perhaps stupid of me to let conscience get the better of common sense: the conflict between ward obligations and the demands of being a committee member is a permanent source of stress for all elected members.

Englefield Green was always depressing; could ever a name have been more inappropriate? It consisted of blocks of flats and maisonettes grouped round an open 'green', one of them a 14-storey point block, which have since been totally demolished. In the mood I was in, it was insupportable. The new part, where, following a clearance scheme, there were houses with bits of garden, was bad enough. Repairs had not been done. Houseproud efforts like fancy fencing round the front door all askew, the little gates hanging off their hinges, a symbol of lost hope. A house where there had been a fire ages ago still stood gaping and derelict. But it was the blocks of flats that really sickened me. Dog dirt on the stairs; human dirt too. Street lights with the guts of the timing device hanging out like the entrails of a corpse on a battlefield. Overflowing bins, unemptied for weeks. Scavenging dogs. And perched on every broken wall, groups of teenagers, Black and white together, doing nothing because there was nothing to do, without hope, unwanted, alienated. All these years I had been a Councillor and had bleated on about the shame of Granby, all to no effect. The sense of doom and failure hung like lead in my heart. There was trouble in the air like the stink from the bins.

And trouble on the streets too. This time it was as near as need be to civil war, cops against citizens, both sides raring to go. The Chief had had time to assemble protective gear and consider his strategy. So too had sundry activists who saw their chance in the general dis-affection. Fearful deeds were done. Petrol bombs were thrown. On the Sunday night, a taxi driver suffered a savage attack from which he has to this day never recovered. In what has become the Ulster tradition, police vehicles were used as a means of dispersal. On the Monday, a man's back was broken following a blow from a police vehicle. Yet again on the Tuesday, more trouble. Early the following morning I was rung by Radio Merseyside for comment: during the night a young local man, David Moore, had been killed in a 'police traffic accident'. I was stunned and could only mumble some reply. But one phrase I was never to be allowed to forget, nor have I ever wanted to. I told the reporter of how I had been round the flats the weekend before, and nothing had changed. For all the drama and the burning and the looting, for all the media fuss and the visits by Ministers, nothing had changed. Not even the bins had been emptied in all those three weeks. I told her that I was not surprised that there had been trouble: indeed '...they would be apathetic... fools ... if they didn't protest.'

Those who heard it for themselves thought nothing of it. It was only when the mass media picked it up and left out the preamble about nothing at all having been done since the first riots, that the 'outrageousness' of what I had said was appreciated. The pressure brought to bear on me to recant was hard and heavy. So too was the misrepresentation of anything I said by way of clarification. No wonder that I was misunderstood and reviled. Yet I had absolutely no doubt as to the stand I had to take. The remark I had made had been a spontaneous expression of the deep anger provoked in me by what I had seen on that leafletting exercise; three weeks on and nothing had changed. 'They' had done nothing. The more I was pressed to withdraw, the more desperate my need to find words which would convey to others the astonishing sense of revelation which I had experienced. That remark was wrenched out of me like a nugget of gold out of some dark mine of feeling. Only, like a nugget, it came out awkward and rough, and it has irritated me ever since that I expressed myself so clumsily. Yet perhaps it should stand as a measure of the despair which engulfed me that I, who have on occasion been complimented by journalists on my 'pretty turn of phrase', should find words fail me on this of all occasions. All my lifetime of belief that patient persistence, persuasion, the reconciliation of opposing views, would eventually bring its due reward — suddenly, all that deserted me and I faced the fact of its failure. I had laboured for all those long years in vain. The bread I had cast upon the waters had been devoured by sharks. The futility of my own endeavours dismayed me. I had tried so hard but I had so evidently got it wrong.

The miracle was that out of that moment of bleakest renunciation of all that my life had stood for, dawned a startling new comprehension of where I had failed. 'It skinned my eyes for me', as a Black writer has put it. It was one of the most profound experiences of my entire life.

The truth that I now faced was that for all the earnestness of my endeavour, the basic premise on which I had worked was fatally flawed. My complacent belief that I stood for the right of the 'meanest he' to play some part in determining his own destiny had been found wanting. I had countenanced the wholesale deprivation of an entire community of their right to be full members of our society. By persuading them to tolerate the imposition of government I had in reality perpetuated their deprivation. I had administered the law all right, totally committed to the belief that if government was efficient and upright everything would be fine. To this day the police parade their dedication to that ideal. But I had completely failed to realise that the law is not relevant to life in Granby and that to enforce it can result in injustice, not justice. The enormity of my offence shocked and shamed me. Suddenly I realised the significance of my own remark that the people of Granby were not even granted the right to have their bins emptied. As a shrewd Black friend once observed, I had till then operated as a twin-set-and-pearls white liberal. I had smugly accepted that I was one of 'Them', justly set in authority over other lesser beings. Unwittingly, I had helped to perpetuate the very injustice which I had declared myself to be committed to ending. Though I have never finally resolved in my own mind the question of whether the resort to violent protest can ever be justified, what was required of me then and there was the open avowal of my own new commitment. I must henceforth truly and genuinely have 'faith in the city'. I must be on the side of those who suffer injustice at the hands of their fellow men. I must bear witness on their behalf.

The storm of abuse which broke over me personally was, of course, hard to bear or even to understand. I had no time to think; it was all I could do to survive each day as it broke. I became the object of a torrent of invective from both sides, the public who were largely pro-police and the extremists who were passionately hostile to them. I was described as a muddling old fool, a dangerous commie who ought to go back to Russia, a nigger lover. It was a revelation. It seemed as if I had become a face at which people could hurl all the emotional sludge stirred up by the riots, all the prejudices and bias, the hate and the fear, the selfishness and the greed. Or is it that there is in all of us a deep well of evil and malice?

I found the invasion of my privacy peculiarly hard to bear. A quote by me was a must for journalists from all over the world. They arrived on the doorstep. They surfaced at my housing surgeries. People stopped me in the street and the market crying out that they had seen me on TV. I gave up going to concerts or the theatre because someone was sure to nail me to the wall with a barrage of argument. I discovered every back alley in the city so that I could avoid walking the main streets. Most devastating of all was the creation by the media of a puppet figure cheerfully dubbed by my grandsons as the Old Witch. Regardless of accuracy, whatever I said or did had to be geared to this other self who moved in on my life like an unwanted and deeply disliked lodger. Yet I came to realise that by personalising the debate, the media did us good service. The mere physical contrast between the Chief and myself constituted a valuable visual aid to what might otherwise have appeared to be an academic discussion.

The redeeming feature was the remarkable number who got the message: how apt the tag for once, for message it certainly was. Some, of course, rejoiced that I of all people, with my mincing middle-class manners, had brought about my own downfall by preaching revolution. Some blessed me for my courage in speaking out for the oppressed. My Labour colleagues gave me quite surprising loyalty. The administration were superb in their personal care for me whatever their private opinions. Most surprising of all was the understanding extended to me by local Black people.

On the basis of first-hand experience of the West Indies, I have always schooled myself to humble acceptance of our failure as a nation to remedy our inheritance of racial prejudice and our continuing assumption of white superiority. Suddenly to find myself acceptable, accepted, forgiven, by these most outcast of people was a revelation of joy in the context of that vast cloud of disapproval, hatred and malice which now shrouded my existence day and night.

Denigration of me and my choice of words certainly enabled many to evade the dreadful lesson of the disturbances, that from the Prime Minister downwards we are only prepared to listen to the cry of the deprived when it takes the form of attacks on our property. Many were prepared to leave it at that. But for me life was henceforth to be dominated by one question: how to put my new found 'conversion' into practice? A vision without hope of achievement is a delusion. Even while I struggled to make sense out of the confusion of mind into which I had been thrown, the urgency of the need for the Authority to make immediate decisions left little time for thought. Our purpose must be to serve the people, not the police. But how?

Part II

4

The Dilemma Discovered

The Prime Minister visited Liverpool on 13 July 1981. My meeting with her was less than pleasing. She was not out to please. Significantly, even though I was Chairman of the Police Authority, I had not originally been included in the list for the VIP meeting at the Town Hall but had managed to insert myself in place of a member absent on holiday. Mrs Thatcher uttered not one word of pity or compassion for our plight. It was plainly our own fault and we were required to show contrition. Each of us was introduced according to our rank and given a few minutes to make a contribution. It always surprised me on such occasions to find that I had anything to say; the depth of my experience in Granby proved an unfailing source and words always came.

When my turn came, without giving me time to utter a solitary word, she launched into a long spiel about our duty to the police. The police must be supported; the police must take decisions; the police were the guardians of law and order. On and on. I bided my time, and then enquired politely, 'In that case, Mrs Thatcher, what is the role of the Police Authority?' I must be one of the rare few who have ever halted her flow of positive exhortation. There was total silence. I could sense her supporting officials willing her to reply. But her concept of law and order permits of no nonsense about policing by consent and she smartly passed on to someone else.

I repeat the story because it sums up so accurately the situation in which we found ourselves following the disturbances. The sacred cow which had previously barred our way had blown up into a monster of prehistoric proportions. No one could conceive of any possible use in the current situation for a collection of elected members. Never mind what the law laid down about the duties of a Police Authority: to all and sundry the police were the last bastion of security in what had suddenly become so frightening a world, and not a word of criticism of them must be uttered. The bits of bother we had previously had with the Chief over the question of who polices the police were swept aside by the flood of emotion roused by the outbreak of such massive disorder on our very own doorstep. There was widespread acceptance of the assumption that policing was police business and politicians must keep out.

All and sundry in the way of VIPs descended on Toxteth but few showed any interest in meeting the Chairman of the Police Authority. My Deputy and I were not invited to join William Whitelaw, the Home Secretary, for lunch at HQ though we managed to attend nevertheless. Timothy Raison, Junior Minister concerned with race relations, spared us only 40 minutes of his time. Michael Heseltine, Minister for Merseyside, proved elusive though he had time for dinner with the Chief Constable. The Chief Inspector of Constabulary came and went without even informing us of his visit. It was hard to argue the toss against such a mixture of indifference as to our existence and outright condemnation of our behaviour. Who were we to insist that we had any right to poke our noses into what was clearly none of our business or to claim that we had anything of value to contribute to a situation which left far greater persons than ourselves aghast?

On the other hand, we could not possibly ignore the passion of hostility against the police, particularly in the Toxteth area. There could be no doubt that to some, at least, policing was felt to be an intolerable imposition of control by an outside force: to talk of consent to such as these was derisory in the light of their experience. Such information as had already come our way suggested that it was the denial of any effective means of securing the redress of what were very real grievances that had led to the explosion of feeling on those nights of violence and that it was surely a proper cause for concern to us as elected representatives. Not that this reaction was confined to Liverpool: I found it deeply disturbing as well as reassuring that my mail included messages of support from all over the country. So much public anxiety could not be ignored; we had to make a response of some sort.

This was no academic debate. All around us public opinion seethed with emotion. Anything and everything was blamed for what had happened in Toxteth. Inner area malaise, police behaviour, the economic system, and much more besides were all thrown in to make one massive hotch-potch. The more explanations as to the cause of the riots that were put forward, the more difficult it was for us to decide on any coherent plan of action. We were all so deeply shocked by what had taken place; as a community, so confused as to what had really happened, what it all really meant. There were rumours and denials, accusations and counter-accusations. The media descended on us from all corners of the earth. The best of them showed a welcome understanding of our position, but others reported with relish what they saw as prime entertainment in the shape of gladiatorial combat between a female termagant and a muscular official. The limelight was hard to bear. I was totally bewildered as to what part the Police Authority or I as its Chairman should play. Mrs Thatcher was not the only person who could find no answer to the question: what then is the role of the Police Authority?

There was no time to think. Maybe the world at large had no use for us but nevertheless, the administration required formal decisions from us as the committee charged with the duty of authorising expenditure. The tension which had previously existed between the Committee and the Chief rapidly escalated when it was reported to us that the Chief had purchased riot gear to the tune of some £53,000 without committee approval, ignoring the fact that the County's Standing Orders provide for decisions to be made in a matter of minutes if circumstances require. With the recent row over the budget still fresh in our minds, we were in no mood to rubber-stamp the purchase of anything so controversial. Nor were we lightly prepared to accept as a charge on the rates liability for compensation for the wholesale destruction of property which had taken place. And who was to pay for the officers from other Forces who had come to our assistance, or for damage done to their vehicles and equipment? The daily pressure for quick response forced us to make instant decisions as we went along but this was no answer to our problem. Were we or were we not rubber stamps? Every item that came before us raised the issue all over again.

The most immediate problem on our plate was what to do about the demand that 'Oxford Must Go'. This continued to gather force in spite of the temporary release of pressure afforded by the disturbances. For my part, though as a representative for Granby, I could not but be inescapably aware of the intensity of the emotion which powered the campaign, yet as a politician, I shrank from giving it outright support without first giving thought to the consequences. It was obvious to me that any attempt to dislodge so powerful a figure as a Chief Constable would call for the most careful political manoeuvring if it was to succeed. There could be no bull-at-a-gate tactics. The Home Secretary had been quick to make it absolutely clear that so far as he was concerned he would never for one moment contemplate the dismissal of a chief officer in response to mob demand. The entire hierarchy of officialdom would be solidly against us. Public opinion would certainly come out strongly in support of the Chief. However, there were others who were all for hurling themselves to a martyr's death on the barricades: they insisted that we demand the Chief's resignation even though there was no hope of securing it. I am myself sceptical of martyrdom as a means of achieving social progress, nor does instant revolution appeal to me as a practical way of bringing about change, but those who differed from me had no such hesitations. Unencumbered by experience, with which I was possibly overloaded, they knew that the police were to blame. They knew that the use of CS gas was not justified. They knew that if only they could get rid of the Chief, the system would be smashed, a favourite phrase.

The push and pull of external pressures and internal differences drove me to the point where I felt almost literally torn to pieces. The pleas from groups like the Community Relations Council for a government inquiry into policing factors during the disturbances and into policing practice generally were indisputable and urgent. Yet it was beyond doubt that the vehemence of those who insisted that 'Oxford Must Go' so muddied the water as to make it certain that the outcome could only be a refusal. The mere fact that we should entertain any doubt as to the rightness of police activity during the riots had already brought a torrent of abuse down on us. I was appalled by the prospect of the all-out confrontation which would ensue if we associated this with a personal attack on the Chief. The way forward, to my mind the only way, lay in working towards a solution which would result in leaving the field clear for a major review of policing policies. I believe that this could have been achieved and that the Authority would have emerged with greatly enhanced prestige had we played our cards this way. As it was, all hope of a negotiated settlement vanished when in mid-August an anti-Oxford march was organised complete with a pig's head wearing a police helmet. Some of my members openly gave it their support. Our credibility went in a flash. No responsible government could yield to that kind of pressure.

I have no doubt that it was that campaign which provided the Home Secretary with a ready excuse for refusing our very reasonable request for a Home Office inquiry into the police response to the disturbances. The use of CS gas for the first time in mainland Britain constituted such an innovation in policing policy that some sort of official investigation was surely called for. All the more so because, as is now known, the Cabinet had in fact been warned by its own think-tank not long before the riots of the troubles to come. We never discovered whether the local Force were advised of this; if so, what of their protestations that the riots took them completely unawares? As it was, the heavy emphasis on the need for an inquiry as a means of proving the 'guilt' of the Chief so weakened the case for a much broader investigation of policing policy in general as to undermine it beyond redemption.

Additionally, the launching of legal proceedings by members of the public against the police for injuries suffered at their hands was used to justify a total embargo on any discussion of complaints in general because of the sub judice rule. With the experience of subsequent years, I have come to believe that we could have challenged this dictate, but the immediate situation was so tangled that this never occurred to us as a practical possibility. Its continued misuse is a loose end which to this day cries out for attention.

All in all, I quickly came to the conclusion that the 'Oxford Must Go' campaign was a dead duck. My miserable experience of the Joint National Conferences at which Police Authority members met with the Association of Chief Police Officers (ACPO) had taught me that ranks of clones stood ready to step into the Chief's shoes should they ever fall vacant. It was the system we had to go for, not any one individual. With reluctance on the part of some, we abandoned the blame game, for the moment at least, and turned instead to trying to get to grips with the question of whether the actual policing of the riots had been adequately handled or not. Nobody could deny that the provision of a competent Force was our legal responsibility but turning words into deeds proved to be exasperatingly difficult. The customary procedure was to ask the Chief for a report but it was apparent that we were miles apart as to what that report should contain. I think he was genuinely at a loss as to how to deal with our request since he regarded it as a blatant intrusion into his personal domain. I recollect that he rang me at one point to demand with some irritation what it was we wanted to know. In the event his report consisted of no more than a handful of pages plus a blow-by-blow chronology of the events which had taken place. The much longer report which he had submitted to Lord Scarman was attached as an appendix though he refused to discuss it with us. What we needed was an evaluation from some other source than that of the officer whose actions were the subject of criticism. With incredulity we realised that no such assistance was available to us. The Home Secretary had flatly refused our plea for an inquiry and his Chief Inspector of Police only paid us the barest of courtesy visits; he had once confided to me that his policy was all for a quiet life. No ACAS type of mechanism existed to which we could turn for help. We were on our own. There was nothing for it but to do it ourselves.

Our first thought had been to 'send for Scarman', he being already deep into his investigation of the Brixton disorders, but this proved to be outside his brief. Alternatively we could have opted for an inquiry of a legal type, as did Greater Manchester. But the more we thought about the idea of bringing in someone from outside the less we were attracted to it. Toxteth had already been subjected to more research into its multiple ills than any similar area in the country. My husband's Department of

Social Science at the University had for years been producing studies of various aspects of local life of which John Mays' *Growing Up In The City* achieved international fame. There had also been numerous projects designed to demonstrate what could or could not be done. What we required was not yet more general analysis of the situation in the inner areas and the cause and cure of the distress thereof, but an investigation tightly geared to the part played by policing. This was the aspect about which there was surprisingly little information. There could be no argument as to where we should start; we were united in our dismay over the ferocity of the hostility displayed against the police in Toxteth. The then Deputy Chief Constable, Peter Wright, had remarked with a kind of stunned disbelief that 'they hated us... they *hated* us... you could see it in their eyes...' By a stroke of inspiration on the part of my Deputy, we decided against a direct approach to selected groups and instead, published an open invitation in the local press.

Come early September we were in business. Night after night, week after week, we made ourselves available to meet anyone who cared to come. The administrative staff laboured away at the servicing of the meetings, putting in untold hours of late duty in a way which reflected the profound concern provoked amongst us all by the riots. The Chief did not attend but his Deputy was present throughout, accepting all that was thrown at him with the courtesy we had come to expect of him. We waited with some anxiety to see if our inquiry would be boycotted by the Black groups but in the event the response was satisfactory once it had been made clear that it was the Authority and not the police who were conducting it. Even so, when I politely introduced our side, some of our visitors flatly refused to respond, and on at least one occasion, showed signs of walking out at that point.

Even I, who had lived with the situation for so many years, was shocked by the extent of the mutual antagonism which was revealed to us. What we heard stunned us. Whether we already had experience of conditions in the inner city or not, all of us who listened were deeply dismayed by the clear evidence of the existence of a whole community of the alienated right in our midst. The thought that policing should be by consent was derisory in the light of what we were told; policing was obviously seen by many to be a form of oppressive control imposed by outsiders with little understanding of life in an inner city area. In particular, the issue of racism pushed itself to the forefront of our consideration in a way which forcibly challenged the long-held belief that racial prejudice was unknown in Merseyside. For some members it was possibly the first time that they had engaged in serious conversation on this sore subject with any of those most directly involved. The overall picture which emerged was not at all what we expected. The hostility was genuine but it was that of a people desperate for help and bitterly resentful of their rejection. Rather to our surprise, considering the recent turmoil, 'without exception all those who talked to us left us in no doubt that they supported the maintenance of law and order and wished to see effective and acceptable policing in their area. It was also clear that they were equally prepared and willing to do all that was possible to bring this about' (*Interim Report on Police/Public Relations*, p. 3). This was, however, qualified by scepticism as to whether the well-meant efforts of the Authority would have any effect.

The scene presented to us by the staff associations was totally different from that described by the community groups. To them, Toxteth was a hotbed of disorder and criminality and must be policed as such, which meant that the policing must often be literally physical. They displayed little comprehension of the stresses and strains of inner city life, arguing that their duty was to enforce the law without regard to the consequences. Their apparent self-confidence was unshaken by their failure to foresee the imminence of trouble or to comprehend the reasons for the outbreak.

All this was received with various degrees of credence on the part of the committee. It was difficult to find any solid ground on which to take up a stand, and we came to the conclusion that the Deputy Chief Constable was right when he suggested that the extraordinary mish-mash of gossip and myth about policing might well be a major reason why the relationship with the public was so poor. Allegations about the extent and abuse of 'sus', for example, or about the fate of individuals taken into custody, swept through the area like wildfire even when they were flatly denied by the police. The build-up of the campaign against the Chief, much of it insecurely grounded on fact as it was, created a monster of superhuman dimensions which obscured the genuine causes of criticism that inspired it.

The police were equally ill-informed. They too appeared to rely on assumptions which were wide open to challenge. Such monitoring as took place was almost wholly conducted on an in-house basis. The last thing Inspectors appeared to do was inspect what was actually going on out on the streets. As for the Public Relations section, this was commonly regarded as existing to protect information rather than to circulate it. The final blow was our discovery that not even the Force, let alone the public, was aware of the existence of the Authority or understood the reason for it.

We were so disturbed by the urgency of the situation we had un-
covered that we issued the *Interim Report on Police/Public Relations* in
October 1981. In it we firmly asserted our own responsibility for securing
satisfactory relationships between Force and public and committed ourselves to a 12-point programme designed 'to promote mutual support and
understanding as the sole basis on which a police force can operate'.
Brave words, but our choice of phrase in the succeeding recommendations conveys the extreme wariness with which past experience had
taught us to tread. We would undertake a survey of the use of stop-and-
search 'in consultation with the Chief Constable'. We remarked with
evident timidity that we would like to make a contribution to the pro-
posed intensive beat scheme in Toxteth. We would 'urgently pursue
with the Chief Constable offers from other agencies to co-operate in
the sharing of experience'. And so on. Our only independent initiative
was the proposal that we should set up some form of police consultation
in Toxteth which in the event proved to be a forerunner to the scheme
for Scarman Forums.

All of this we presented in the form of a single package based on the
assumption that we and the police would forthwith set about our various
tasks on a basis of partnership. In the euphoric aftermath of the riots we
took this for granted and the amiable reaction of the Chief did nothing
to alert us to our misapprehension. It is significant, however, that we
thought it necessary to conclude with an invitation to the Chief to discuss
with my Deputy and myself 'how best to ensure that the conclusions of
the report are energetically pursued so that the Committee's acceptance
of its responsibility for the continuing improvement of police/public
relations can be maintained.' ˙

Our final report was ready by December 1981. Its title is significant of
of the direction in which we were moving: *The Merseyside Disturbances
— The Role and Responsibilities of the Police Authority*. In so far as it
attempted to weigh up the service provided by the local Force, much of
what we had to say was common to all the similar reports produced elsewhere; the need for better training, more officers on the beat, and so on.
But our report differed from those prepared by others in one important
respect, that it was directed at the Police Authority and not the police.
However fumbling our thinking, it was in fact a first attempt to spell out
the responsibilities of a Police Authority not merely as distinct from those
of a Chief Constable but as being different in kind. We had obviously
acquired a much clearer grasp of the fact that we were not there to run
the Force but to see to it that it was run, and to the satisfaction of the
public we represented.

The recommendations we put forward over the vexed question of the use of plastic bullets illustrates this new maturity on our part. We had never discussed the policing of public disorder situations with the Chief before the disturbances and he had been left to his own devices. Belatedly, we now placed on record our total opposition to the use of plastic bullets as instruments of crowd control, and, without attempting to overrule his professional judgment, made it clear that we would hold the Chief accountable for the consequences should he decide to go against our policy. This was progress so far as it went but the quarrelling with the Chief in recent years left us uneasy. Suppose, as seemed all too probable, he argued that the responsibility for the control of incidents of disorder had been delegated by us to him and that he must therefore be left free to get on with his job as best he could. No one could possibly suggest that the policing of a riot could be controlled by a committee. What then of our right to responsibility?

The Chief appeared to accept all that we had to say with tolerance but quite quickly we became aware of a defeating sense of frustration. Our 12-point programme sank from sight like a stone in a pond. As early as December, we recorded our deep dismay that 'in spite of all our earnest endeavours to resolve the many issues arising from the disturbances, the exercise has not succeeded in every respect'. The police seemed quite willing to listen to anything we had to say, though some did not conceal their doubts as to its value, but when it came to putting ideas into practice, that was 'operational' and therefore their exclusive responsibility. Any attempt by us to play a more active part than that of a police admiration society was resented as being highly improper interference, doubly undesirable because we were politicians. This opposition seldom took the form of outright rejection of any suggestions we might make but it was none the less effective. Somehow, it was the Lord Lieutenant, complete with sword, who acted as figurehead when occasion demanded. Somehow, it was the Chief Constable who received the golden key from the contractors on the completion of the new headquarters building. Somehow, attempts to inform ourselves by making contact with anyone but the top command came to nothing. Somehow, decisions were taken without reference to the Committee. The message was clear. There was simply no room in the system for us.

Slowly it dawned on us that the trouble was not that the Force was indifferent to the need for action or was lacking in desire to improve the service, far from it; but that it completely failed to see it as any business of ours. We were back with our old dilemma: who was responsible for what? Whether it was done consciously or not, we were made

to feel that we were unwelcome intruders. Whatever we turned our attention to, the police were already in occupation. The most radical amongst
us had never dreamed of so comprehensive a system of workers' control.
Selection, training, the deployment of resources, conditions of service,
even the extent to which the police should be accountable to us for what
they did, nowhere could we find so much as a toe-hold. Activists made
great play of the claim that the police were out of control. The much more
chilling truth was that it was we who were, literally, out of control.

It would be tedious to detail the endless bickering which followed. The
mutual mistrust between members and Force developed into an open
conflict which drove the two sides to take up ever more extreme positions.
The habitual suspicion of politicians on the part of the Force was stoked
up by the activities of the Militant-controlled Liverpool City Council to
such a degree as to lead the police to oppose any form of democratic
scrutiny. Some quite extravagant claims were made by officers at all
levels. The Police Authority existed only to advise; it was for the police
alone to decide whether they would take that advice. The job of the
Authority was simply to 'pay up and shut up'. An officer newly appointed
to high command warned me that though he would answer any questions I
put to him, within reason — 'reason' being for him to determine — he
would never voluntarily tell me anything about police operations. This
attitude was not specific to Merseyside: ACPO representatives across the
country expressed outrage against what they held to be political interference and their lead was followed with hysterical zeal by the Federation
to the point at which it eventually, some years later, led them to declare
that they would find it difficult to serve under a Labour government
should one be elected. Even the Superintendents' Association, on occasion, lost their normal cool.

Painful experience quickly taught us that guerrilla warfare as a means of
snatching back random bits and pieces of the authority the police had
acquired was a game we were bound to lose. The cards were stacked
against us right from the start. Councillors as part-time, voluntary workers
had not a hope of exercising effective day-to-day control over so complex
an organisation. Even my most radical members came to accept this: most
of us were convinced that it would not be desirable even if it were possible. Though we remained firmly committed to the belief that ultimate
responsibility must remain vested in the people, for practical purposes we
ourselves must be prepared to keep out of the actual running of the Force.
We were never given credit for this sensible conclusion so blinded were our

critics by the utterances of extremists elsewhere who demanded control, complete control, and nothing less than control.

Actually this was not an easy thought to accept, and the idea that councillors are not there to run a public service but to see that it is run was one not readily assimilated. Councillors are locked into the local government system by force of habit every bit as tightly as are the police in their professional strait-jacket. It was difficult to believe that what was required of us was that we should abandon our long tradition of commitment to the administration of services which has in the past been so rewarding both to the public and to the individuals concerned.

Still more difficult to accept was the thought that if we followed the line that the operation of the Force must be delegated to the professionals, we would have to re-think the reason for our own existence. There was an unforgettable moment at a National Conference when a Councillor cried out in anguish that if we handed management over to the Force, 'What is there left for us to do?' What indeed! It was a bleak prospect which we were understandably reluctant to consider, especially in view of the continuing volume of protests against policing policies in areas like Toxteth. Nevertheless it was a theme which we proceeded to pursue with considerable energy. Lord Scarman accepted our invitation to come north to meet us. My Deputy and I went to see the Home Secretary to discuss our difficulties as to the role of the Authority. The Chief Inspector found time to come and see us. We entered into a fiery debate with the 'Minister for Merseyside', who argued that his remit did not cover policing even though his objective was to secure co-ordination between government services. The Chairman of the Police Complaints Board discussed with us the whole system of complaints and the necessity for changes. The argument we put to each in turn was that it was all very well to argue that authority to run the Force had been delegated to the Chief and no one must interfere with his command, but it was quite unacceptable to suggest that this set him free from his obligation to account to us as elected representatives for his stewardship. All we had heard in criticism of the complaints system revolved round the fact that the police investigated complaints against themselves. To leave it to them to check the 'account' of their own activities made no sense to the man in the street, still less to us as his elected representatives.

In the light of the spate of discussion about policing which has subsequently taken place, it is difficult to recapture the bewilderment with which we contemplated our predicament. We had gone along with the delegation of authority to our professional staff. We had accepted that we must be extremely wary of interfering with their autonomy in enforcing the law. Yet out of these two rights had come what we were sure was the wrong, that by so doing we had forfeited our own right to responsibility. We were in business to represent the interests of the customers whom the service existed to serve. They had expressed their dissatisfaction in unmistakable terms. Yet we seemed to be helpless to respond to any practical effect. Some urged us to fight to the death. Many lost heart, believing that our dilemma was beyond resolution. Was the conflict between us really irreconcilable or was there a way out? Did we seriously believe that the partnership policing we had so bravely talked about in our report on the riots was a practical possibility in view of the claim to autonomy so obstinately defended by the police as a profession?

Relations between us and the Force continued to deteriorate as opinions hardened. We began to take up positions in hostile camps with no common ground between us, barely on shouting terms across the no man's land which separated us. What developed to my distress was a blatant struggle for power which on occasion excluded all rational thought. There were many who advised us that the most we could hope for was to achieve a relationship with the Force on a grace-and-favour basis. The magistrates skirmished helplessly on the fringes, one taking his antagonism to me personally so far that ultimately a solicitor's letter of warning had to be sent.

Scarman's report on the Brixton disorders appeared just as our own inquiry finished and we were gratified to find that much of what we had to say was in accordance with his findings. He, too, argued that though it was a basic principle that the police must be independent so far as the enforcement of the law was concerned, it was equally essential that they should be accountable to the people if public support or 'consent' was to be secured. He, too, attributed the hostility which the police encountered to the fact that there was 'no satisfactory or sufficient link between accountability and consultation' (p. 129). There was, however, one major point of difference between us in that Scarman resolutely refused to discuss the political implications of what he was saying. Perhaps because he was not a practising politician he was content to leave it to the police to remedy the situation; improved consultation on their part and goodwill all round would be sufficient to ensure effective accountability. In the light of experience, we regarded this as totally unrealistic. However, our own inquiry had made us so acutely conscious of the dangers of the gulf between police and policed that we were not prepared to condemn his proposals outright. To meet the public would be as good a starting point as any from which to set out in search of accountability. Faced with the implacable obstruction by the police of any interference on our part, what alternative had we?

5

We Meet the People

Beyond a rather vague idea that consultation was a Good Thing, we had no clear intention in seeking to meet the public other than that police and people should be persuaded to talk to each other instead of throwing petrol bombs and banging plastic shields as their only means of communication. When John Alderson, the then Chief Constable of the Devon Force, first launched his scheme for community liaison in the early 1970s as a specific style of policing, we had shared the general scepticism, regarding it as yet òne more example of do-good liberalism. Our Chief stoutly declared that all policing must of necessity be of that ilk and anyhow, we on Merseyside had been well into the business of community relations long before Devon or Handsworth. Liverpool had in fact pioneered the Juvenile Liaison Scheme as far back as 1946 and since then had developed a scheme for Assistant Community Liaison Officers (ACLOs) who were attached to local stations to serve as contacts with the surrounding community.

However, hard pressed as we were to find some answer to the urgent public demand for action, whether in Toxteth or elsewhere in the County, the idea of 'community policing' took on a new look. What was meant by the label was never made clear. Judging by the Chief's reports and by the discussions at our public meetings, community policing consisted of a compound of bobbies-on-the-beat, softly softly or 'sensitive' tactics in dealing with offenders, and a more genial approach to the public in general. The public wasted no time on definitions; they knew what they wanted. 'Why can't we have nice policemen like the ones we had during the riots who came from other Forces?' we were asked. It was happily assumed that this medley of need was what 'community policing' stood for and enthusiasm for it spread like wildfire.

The fog of words concealed an abyss into which we duly plunged. Too many people cherished too many different expectations for there to be any hope that they could all be satisfied. The lack of agreement between ourselves and the Force certainly compounded the existing discord over what was political and what was operational. So far as we as a committee were concerned, the setting up of consultative machinery was the only aspect of community policing where we had any room for manoeuvre in our own right; everything else seemed to be an intrusion on operational territory. Fortunately for us, Scarman had specifically recommended that the provision of opportunities for public consultation should be a statutory duty of Police Authorities so we homed in on it without more ado. Why ACPO let this slip through without stronger opposition I have never understood; possibly they thought it a harmless by-pass up which we could be allowed to stray without getting into mischief.

The ground had already been prepared for us by the County-wide series of meetings we had held in response to the predictable protests that Toxteth seemed to be claiming more than its fair share of the attention and of the available resources. Everywhere we went we had encountered a quite desperate need to meet 'Them' and to tell those in authority what was thought of the services they rendered. Our protests that we were only there to talk about policing were swept to one side; the audiences had little patience with the artificial boundaries laid down by bureaucrats. There were demands for Something To Be Done about street lighting, emptying the bins, youth clubs, housing; the list was endless. The sense of sheer frustration against 'Them' and their imposition of control over daily life spilled over at every meeting. Government by consent hardly seemed an appropriate description. The separation of government from governed, police from policed showed up as a fact of daily life, deeply resented and as dangerous as a hidden minefield.

The Chief saw 'the Circus', as we were called, as doing no more than providing opportunities for police-bashing and did not hesitate to say so. But to those of us who had actually attended the meetings, it was apparent that they met a long-stifled need to secure the redress of grievances against a faceless bureaucracy, which included the police. The first series of meetings had convinced us that consultation was a worthwhile exercise if only for our own benefit, and we therefore welcomed Scarman's recommendation. However, the proposal that there should be a core committee as the centrepiece of each Forum called for thought. Constitution-mongering broke over us in a big way and valuable time was wasted. The more we reflected on the practical difficulties of choosing representatives for these committees from the profusion of voluntary groups which flourish so exuberantly on Merseyside and particularly in Toxteth, the more perilous any kind of selectivity became. Not only would it land us in a quagmire of difficulty as between the various sects and races but it would defeat our very object. What we wanted was some means of easy and open access by anybody and everybody who used the service to those who provided it. Committees are, by definition, exclusive.

In the end I lost such limited patience as I possess. Unlike most other Authorities, we decided to abandon formalities and go for open meetings without any kind of set structure. Our only stipulations were that the meetings should not take place on police premises and that the Chair should not be taken by a police officer. Instead we thought it vital that the Chair should be occupied by a member of the Authority in order that the Forums should be assured of having a hotline to the main committee. Misguidedly, I thought, the magistrates opted out, which increased the burden for the rest of us and on my Deputy in particular. A Community Liaison Sub-committee was set up under the Chairmanship of my Deputy to co-ordinate all this activity and an extra member added to our administrative staff to do the organising. Thus what are now known as Scarman Forums came into being; public meetings held quarterly in each of the 27 sub-divisions. The first was held in Birkenhead in 1982.

In theory this was all fine and dandy and much uplifting talk was had about the scheme being based on a twinning of our resources with those of the Force. In practice this never materialised. Once more the barrier reef of the demarcation dispute blocked our path. The Force would play its part and do its duty but there could be no sharing of responsibility for any matters which called for action; which being interpreted, meant that we were to have no say in any follow-up to the consultations. We tried to avoid separation by briefing our administrator that he was to co-operate with his opposite number in the Force but that was as far as it ever went. On rare occasions and at our request we met as a group the Superintendents who were the key figures in the Forums but the atmosphere tended to be chilly, if not hostile, and the etiquette of the hierarchy prevented the free speech which might have cleared the air. 'Twinning' hardly seemed the appropriate word; though on the ground, I hasten to add, individuals achieved excellent relationships as happened in my own area in Granby.

We had in effect taken our first step towards becoming an independent executive committee rather than being an advisory body dependent on the goodwill of the police. This change was an inevitable consequence of the Criminal Justice Act which stipulated that public consultations were our responsibility but it was one which introduced a new and powerful factor for discord into the already unhappy relationship between Chief and Authority. A rather ludicrous 'His' and 'Hers' situation developed at times with the Chief drawing a hard line between what he saw as his responsibility and what was ours.

Overall, it took us time to get into our stride. It proved difficult to break out of the customary pattern of public meetings; a platform party cocked up on a dais, neat regiments of chairs far in excess of what were likely to be required, and time-wasting nit-picking over the minutes of the last meeting. Sometimes exception was taken to the presence of either too many officers or too few. Whether they should wear uniform and sit up front or turn up in civvies and sit informally amongst the audience was another recurrent subject for criticism. Participation by policemen who happened to be local residents and saw the Forum as an opportunity to air their own grievances against the top command created a stir on one occasion. Some police and politicians found it difficult to talk in a relaxed way with the public but others proved to be naturals at the job. I remember with particular relish a packed meeting in the Haydock Council Chamber where the Police Superintendent was a local lad known to all by his first name. The friendly ribaldry with which he was treated and with which he retaliated concealed a depth of common concern about local problems which carried the discussion far into the night. The official visiting party put on their coats and left them to it.

Surprisingly few of those involved seemed to have any grasp of the real implications of consultation as an aspect of accountability. The endless street meetings and gatherings of residents in Granby had long since convinced me of the potential of ordinary people for responsible discussion but this was a belief that not all shared with me, especially when applied to policing. Political rallies were one thing but cultivating an attitude of respect towards consumers was a commercial art with which neither police nor public were familiar. It was noticeable that on housing estates where there was an established community centre, the standard of political expertise was sometimes impressive. Not only was a warm welcome extended to those who attended, with free cups of tea and kind words, but the audience was at ease in the format of a public meeting, saying their piece with pith and vigour. Compared with the reserve-stricken gatherings in some of the suburbs, the contrast was revealing.

Whatever the deficiencies of the Forums as a consultative exercise, it was evident that the public found the insight into the working of the Force a fascinating experience. The presentation of an inside view of life as a police officer provided a useful way of conveying to the public the practicalities of policing, although one officer who was outstandingly good at it expressed resentment at having to play the part of public entertainer. Merely to meet a 'boss' figure in the flesh brought a sense of assurance that there was actually somebody there who would listen. That apart, I realised that what we had done was to devise an alternative to the complaints system. The Chief was quite right when he tartly remarked that the meetings were simply occasions for criticising the Force but we disagreed that this was something to be deplored. The opportunity to make a complaint face to face with an officer of sufficient status to make a response there and then was obviously appreciated, all the more because the presence of an audience provided moral and often enthusiastic support. Complaints about 'trivial' incidents were often far better handled by an informal few words with the Super at the end of the meeting than by the rigmarole of the official procedure. What was even more welcome was the chance to have a go at the arrangements for policing a locality or even a particular street against which the official system provides no scope for complaint. These exchanges, though pretty forthright, were mutually beneficial and probably account for the continued attendance as the years go by.

All this was to the good and greatly to the credit of the Force. Undoubtedly this was public relations work in the best sense of the word. But was it accountability? As time passed, the first flush of satisfaction began to give way to a more doubtful approach on our part. All went well so long as it was within the power of the local police to make an immediate and effective response. There was, for example, the dockside meeting chaired by my Deputy, where a crowd of angry mothers turned up, protesting against what they regarded as a savage sentence imposed by the Courts on one of their lads. This developed into a general and spirited complaint against the police for harassing local youngsters; it was said that they prowled the area in Task Force vehicles and grabbed any young person in sight for no reason other than some trumped-up query about stealing cars. The Superintendent was a traditional British bobby and he took this hostility on the part of his flock very much to heart. He is said to have gone straight back to his station and told his officers that if he caught any of them in that neighbourhood on wheels, he would have them up on a discipline charge. However he did it, the next Forum was a positively embarrassing occasion, so fulsome were the tributes to the police.

The significance of this incident was of course that, without realising it, the public had effectively 'controlled' the police. But all too often the unfortunate Chairman and Superintendent were faced with the painful necessity of reporting back that no action could or would be taken. The reasons varied. Some were straightforward and involved factors such as the financial difficulties between the County and the government but others were less easy to explain. Sometimes Headquarters took on all the characteristics of 'Them', faceless bureaucrats whose decisions were often incomprehensible to us at the front line, be we police or public. Frequently, I must admit, it was some decision by the Authority which roused indignation and disbelief. Politicians certainly came in for a lot of flak.

The situation was complicated by the police embargo on the discussion of anything remotely connected with politics. At the mere mention of the word they shied away like frightened horses. Distressed parents who wanted more effective steps to be taken against drug pushers, or angry shopkeepers who felt that they were not getting value for the high price they paid for policing, were not content with this. They wanted action, yet the action they demanded almost invariably brought out into the daylight the sharp differences between the Authority and the Chief which on occasion developed into an exchange of veiled animosity between us and whichever senior officer was present. People found it hard to believe that a body as powerful as a Police Authority must surely be could nevertheless be incapable of ensuring that its wishes were carried out. It was difficult to explain to them that 'HQ' had always to be consulted and that their edict was final. No local officers ever broke rank except for the rare few.

The walking of this particular tightrope called for a high degree of skill if the decencies were to be observed. It was important not to shake public confidence in the police by appearing to be disloyal to our own Force, yet equally necessary to defend ourselves against criticism by the audience. The theory that having a member of the Authority in the Chair at every Forum would ensure a hotline of communication with the main committee and so guarantee a response proved to be of little use. Those Councillors who sought to raise matters on behalf of their Forums at the Authority's meetings were defeated by the police's bland assurance that the matter had been referred to the appropriate department and would receive attention.

Our own diminishing role troubled us; our presence at meetings seemed to be increasingly a fringe benefit. We did our best to improve our rather amateur performance as community workers and made efforts to increase attendances by better advertising, finding more acceptable premises and making the agendas less formal and more interesting. But insidiously, disillusionment began to seep through us. Having to face even a handful of local residents at a Forum without any capacity to respond to their demands was disheartening to the point where we began to feel that the whole exercise was pointless so far as we were concerned. It was the police the public wanted to meet, not us. The police could do something about the smaller annoyances raised by the residents. But when it came to a cry for more bobbies on the beat, which involved money, they smartly fielded the ball to us. And we were unable to respond. What did we think we were doing, toiling round a succession of school halls and community centres on dark winter nights to meet the comparative few who displayed the faintest interest in our presence in their midst?

By now beginning to grasp that accountability went far beyond the exchange of information as practised at the Forums, we set out to try to expand our original intention across a much broader front. We opened up every possible committee to public attendance. We tried to cultivate the media instead of shunning them, slowly coming to recognise their value in spreading information and encouraging interest and comment even if it was frequently directed against ourselves. Any hint that I would seek the help of the media proved to be a powerful lever in extracting information from the police. It seemed a useful idea to invite the District Councils and the Magistrates' Committees to discuss with us the service we provided but we were rebuffed. The Justices made no effort to conceal their hostility, spelling out in language which startled our administrators that they regarded our efforts as interference in the law and me personally as public enemy number one. The Councils were still resentful of the mere existence of the County Council and wanted nothing to do with 'Big Brother'. Others, however, notably the Probation service, were generous in their response to any approach by us.

Believing that to make a complaint was not an anti-police gesture but a perfectly proper means of calling an officer to account, we put a lot of thought into the working of the official complaints system. After the Kelly case, we had pioneered the setting up of a confidential sub-committee to which the Chief could report on cases even though they might be the subject of investigation and therefore held to be sub judice. This rather surprising concession on his part was doubtless a response to the savage criticism directed against him at that time. This openness on the part of the Chief was opposed by some members of ACPO, one of whom threatened to take the Chief to court. It is to the credit of the Councillors that in all the years of my experience, information was never once leaked by any member of this committee. Its value was that questions raised at the main committee about complaints could be directed to Councillors who were on the sub-committee and whose assurances might attract more credit than those of the Chief in cases where mutual trust was lacking.

Beyond this, the sub-committee made little progress for the familiar reasons. Discussion of the activities of the Special Branch was banned except for the remarkable occasion when the Chief attended a meeting in person to describe to us his position in regard to matters of national security. Information about what happened to officers charged under the Discipline Code was refused. Anything to do with detainees held under the Prevention of Terrorism Act was also barred. Yet all of these were matters of public concern about which secrecy bred damaging suspicion. Our attempts to by-pass the criticism that the police investigated complaints against themselves by constructing a kind of local ombudsman scheme were flatly opposed. When as a fall-back we encouraged the Citizens' Advice Bureau to set up what might be described as an outreach advisory service this too failed to secure police approval, although offence was taken when they were not invited to a press conference because of their declared opposition.

The jewel in our crown was the scheme for Lay Visitors, members of the public authorised to pay visits to any police station at any time of the day or night without prior warning, to those in custody. After much anxious thought on the part of the police which led to tedious delays and our consequent omission from the Home Office list of pilot projects, we decided to go ahead regardless. Guided by my Deputy, we again resorted to an advertisement in the local papers, inviting volunteers. A satisfactory cross-section of the public responded and was duly trained. Only a handful were rejected by the police on grounds laid down by mutual agreement. I suspect that a number of us were surprised to find that the gutters in the Stations did not run with blood. I myself made a special effort to visit one which had a peculiarly hairy reputation. I went in the middle of the night on a Saturday, only to find a calm which would have been a credit to a nursing home. Reassuring though this undoubtedly was — and the police visibly relaxed when they found that we were amiably disposed — there were complaints that the warmth of the welcome extended to us at some Stations was in danger of making the visits too cosy. I found the opportunity for an informal chat with the officer on duty over a mug of tea was often more rewarding than the meeting with someone in custody.

For all that, we quickly became aware that we faced the identical issue which had cropped up in connection with the Forums. To what extent, if at all, could Lay Visitors actually influence any situation that they felt called for attention? This was important if their role was to be seen as anything more than that of ineffectual rubber stamps. The question took on a special urgency regarding those held under the Prevention of Terrorism Act (PTA) who were housed in the old Cheapside Bridewell in Dale Street. Efforts had been made for years to rid ourselves of this Napoleonic fortress but it was still in use, and each time PTA detainees were kept there, groups gathered outside its black walls to sing protest songs. This added melodrama to the request that we should be permitted to visit cases in this category as well as those more usually incarcerated there but this met with only a grudging response, the Chief regarding it as entirely a matter for his discretion.

A similar fate befell our efforts to incorporate the ACLOs in our scheme. They were certainly effective in winning friends for the police and

as a public relations exercise good work was often done. They had made a
useful beginning even before 1981 on the difficult question of race relations and I was one of a number of local people who were invited to take
seminars at the Training College. But as those who talked with us during
our inquiry bluntly commented, neither constables nor community were
under any delusions as to the capacity of the ACLOs to do anything more
than sympathise. They might convey to their superiors the opinions and
feelings of local people but they were totally unable to affect the subsequent decision. Indeed the fact that an ACLO was as powerless as the
people he sought to help endeared him to them; he so evidently shared
their frustration.

The ACLO we had for years in Granby was typical of the best of them.
Known affectionately as 'Our Tom', he had all the virtues of the traditional British bobby; a wise, kindly father-figure who was a visible re-
minder to us all that we must Be Good. He dressed up as Father Christmas
at so many parties that we almost came to believe that he was the old
man in policeman's guise. He grieved with us over our moral dilemma
when members of a youth club were discovered to be on drugs or going
shop-lifting; should they be reported to the police or were we entitled to
deal with them by other means? He exercised a masterly discretion as to
his own obligations in such situations. Alas, poor Tom. A change of wind
at HQ dictated that in future all information picked up in the course of
being friendly must necessarily be fed to a central collator. End of Tom,
who was henceforth kennelled behind the counter of a small sub-station.
The doors of the youth centre slammed shut; they wanted no police spy at
their deliberations and to this day, contact with the police is minimal.

It was a disappointment to find that the ACLOs were not encouraged
to play the leading role at the Forums for which we felt that they were
peculiarly well-fitted. When, later, the Home Watch scheme was floated
as a joint endeavour between police and public, our efforts to relate this to
the Forums were also rebuffed on the grounds that Home Watch was
operational and therefore not Police Authority business. The opportunities
for Lay Visitors to report directly to their local Forums were not always
pursued. It seemed to us that all these developments would have been far
more effective if they had been co-ordinated into a single programme but I
never dared to confide to any but my closest colleagues that the inspiration behind the programme we devised came from my experience of
community development in the West Indies and Southern Africa. The so-
called 'barefoot' approach is specifically designed to meet the need for the
government to support and strengthen the community in its endeavours to
assume responsibility for its own well-being. It would be a mockery to

apply the idea of going barefoot to our well-heeled officers but it would also be a serious misrepresentation. To go barefoot is not merely a gesture of association with those who are poor but is a traditional mark of respect of long standing. Could there be a better definition of community policing?

Apart from the use of the word barefoot, the practice was in fact already well-established in Granby. There had long been a Detached Youth Worker Scheme in the area adjacent to Granby. Two 'detached priests' actually lived and worked right on our doorstep. The Granby Street Junior School had appointed liaison workers especially to bring school and parents together. There was a remarkable scheme for the employment of young Blacks from the local community as auxiliaries to the probation service. There was also the never-to-be-forgotten experiment by the Corporation under which district officers were appointed on an area basis, with money in their pockets, to act directly with residents in securing the clearing of blocked gullies and the removal of old sofas and builders' rubbish. These were all 'barefoot' in that their prime concern was to place themselves at the service of the people by working alongside them. They were 'on our side'.

To talk in this way might seem too far-fetched even for an idealist but on reflection I took courage. After all, what were our Specials and our ACLOs but just such a species? What of Lay Visitors and Forums and Home Watch? It was to the task of knitting all of these into a co-ordinated 'barefoot' programme which was formally as well as practically connected with the rest of the Force's work that the Community Liaison sub-committee under the leadership of my Deputy bravely committed itself.

The Chief Constable had meanwhile been pursuing a quite different strategy under the heading of community policing. Never one to drag his feet when opportunity knocked, he had moved smartly into action following the disturbances. Before any of us had had time to think, perhaps before he himself had done so, and seeing little merit in our plans to meet the public, he pursued his own line of advance. Early in the month following the riots he organised a meeting with invited representatives of community groups in the Law Department of the University. Though geographically handy, we were surprised to find that this 'foreign territory' was regarded as a suitable venue for consultation with the people of Liverpool 8. Unhappily a fair proportion of the community were in no mood to be consulted being then occupied in the vigorous promotion of the 'Oxford Must Go' campaign. A boycott was smartly organised. Ruefully I found myself as Chairman of the Authority having to make at least minimally approving noises in public although in private I winced at what seemed to me to be the ineptness of it all. I tried to offer advice but consultation apparently did not extend to the Chairman of the Authority despite my long life as a local Councillor and my professional experience as a community worker. In the event I was embarrassed to find myself cheered with cries of 'Margaret is our leader' as I entered the building whilst the Chief was booed and efforts made to bounce his car. I played no part in the proceedings, the Archbishop having been invited by the Chief to take the Chair, a point which did not pass unnoticed. Of those who attended nobody spoke out of turn and so little was achieved.

This was followed by a second equally unprofitable meeting held on a cold December night in a draughty ill-lit hall in the City Centre, far too big for the small number of the well-meaning who attended, too few of whom ever set foot in Toxteth. The Archbishop again took the Chair. The meeting was informed that a pilot project (subsequently known as the Toxteth Section) would begin in a few weeks time for intensive beat policing in the area bordering on Upper Parliament Street, where the rioting had been at its worst. The beats would be manned by hand-picked volunteers so far as possible, who, it was hoped, would stay for a couple of years in order that they might become known in the neighbourhood. What locals insisted on calling the Task Force, always regarded as marauders, would only be permitted to enter the area at the request of senior officers. A map was produced showing the exact boundaries of the area to be covered. Comment was invited but was not forthcoming to any noticeable extent. Though residents had not been involved in the preparation of the plan, they were grateful enough, and willing to take the half-loaf offered. There was certainly appreciation of the courage of the officers who volunteered to patrol the very streets which had so lately been the scene of unparalleled hostility. This was accepted as proof positive of their commitment. Our hopes that we ourselves might be permitted to play some part in monitoring the project came to nothing.

Whatever antagonism continued against the police — and it is perhaps endemic in areas of high stress — it was generally conceded that the project provided an invaluable period of stability. The first couple of years after the riots went by far better than could have been expected though the media hovered like carrion crows on each anniversary of those July days. Trouble spluttered into flame from time to time but there was at least a guarded willingness to 'give Scarman a chance' on the part of a fair proportion of local residents.

This stability could only be temporary. People were prepared to wait and see what came of the promises made after the riots, but not indefinitely.

For all the undoubted efforts of at least some of the police, for all the programmes of aid organised by Heseltine, the Minister for Merseyside, nothing had changed. Crime escalated, and there was laughter over a report that burglary in the streets patrolled by the beat bobbies had risen surprisingly. The disillusionment was all the harder to bear because expectations had been so high. Some quite openly told me that since the troubles, they had given me and my kind a chance to play it our way but they were tired of waiting. Trouble on the streets became common. It was borne in on us that the Toxteth scheme was a one-off. What had been intended to be a pilot project designed to explore the viability of community policing as a universal policy had turned into a scheme specifically directed towards the imposition of control over what was regarded as a particularly unruly community. The policing of Toxteth had become a strictly operational matter which must be kept free of outside interference. In the dictionary of policing, consultation and interference seemed to be one and the same thing, and equally undesirable if practised by us.

Baffled and disillusioned by the apparent failure of community policing to produce results, as increasingly we were ourselves, the one thing the public now wanted was more bobbies on the beat, in such numbers that every time they looked out of the window they would see one passing by. The Chief visibly wearied of repeating for the umpteenth time the arguments as to the impracticality/undesirability/ineffectiveness of what was being asked for. In vain we offered explanations to those who attended the Forums. Technology required a new style of highly centralised command-and-control capable of a quick response to calls for help. Our audiences were not interested. It was in their opinion absurd that they should have to call a Liverpool number when they themselves lived in the outer suburbs and wanted to contact a local officer. Academic inquiries had indicated that the chance of a policeman passing by at the moment when a crime was about to be committed was remote to the point of utter improbability; our customers were not impressed. Home Office research had demonstrated that in any case, an increase in the number of officers on the beat had no identifiable effect on the crime rate; that met with a blanket refusal to be convinced. The cost would be phenomenal even if we could secure Home Office approval for the necessary increase in the size of the Force; our public happily chorused their willingness to pay regardless. Undeterred, they nagged on at us, got up petitions, wrote letters to the papers, rang me up in the middle of the night, had questions asked in the House of Commons.

The pressure was hard to resist if for no other reason than that politicians learn to respect the hunches of their constituents; however exasperating they may be, they are often an invaluable indication of some point of stress which is not apparent to the observer. Years ago we had lost contact with the public by allowing the gush of enthusiasm for technology on the part of our professional advisers to result in the closure of small local stations. The sáme fate, it dawned on us, now threatened the very existence of the bobby on the beat. His greatest asset, his freedom to exercise his own discretion, had already been undermined by his subjection to remote control by radio. A year or so later, as our term of office neared its conclusion, the Chief advised us to our considerable dismay that the numbers allocated to this duty were lower than they had been when we first came on the scene. The protection and promotion of this dying species came to take pride of place in our strategy. To the profession, beat bobbies might be the lowest of the low, situated on the bottom rung of the ladder up which every self-respecting constable must make speed to clamber. To us, they were our frontline representatives, key figures in local life, visible about the streets and easily accessible. We even coined the phrase 'visible policing' to encapsulate our intention.

Once more we were into confrontation. The Chief protested that to shift large numbers of officers from specialist departments such as the CID to beat work would involve a radical redeployment of manpower and resources far beyond anything he was prepared to consider. It would stand the entire system on its head. We had come full circle and were back where we had started. Scarman was right; consultation and accountability had parted company. Whatever we tried to do to bring them together had brought us into head-on collision with the apparently insurmountable obstacle of the autonomy of the Force. Against that, what price accountability? Could it be that the fault lay in us, as our critics suggested; that the Authority on which we served had so dismally failed to ensure that its wishes were carried out?

6
The Search for Accountability

When, as the Labour majority, we took office in 1981, the row over who polices the police had already waxed so loud and lasted so long that it had obscured all grasp of what the argument was really about. Glib tribute was paid to accountability as an idea but, as we were to discover, the rhetoric concealed profound hostility to its real implications — which only charity impelled me to attribute to ignorance. The theory of accountability was generally taken for granted. Of necessity in the mass society of today, there must be massive delegation of authority to the faceless regiment of administrators and specialists whom we lump together in casual conversation as 'Them'. This delegation is, of course, subject to the one irrefutable condition that those to whom power is delegated shall be accountable for their stewardship.

So far, so good. It was when we tried to put principle into practice that we ran into difficulty because this raised the whole issue of whether our existing powers were adequate or whether there was nothing for it but to go for fresh legislation. The police held that having delegated unusually extensive powers to them, this was the end of our involvement in the matter. From then on they were solely accountable to the law; their obligation to us would consist of no more than what came to be called 'information accountability'. They would tell us anything we chose to ask but they reserved the right to refuse if, in their opinion, not ours, revelation would not be in the public interest. Scarman notwithstanding, they saw no reason for any change in the accepted practice and were indeed filled with apprehension at the prospect.

To us as Councillors, products of local government, this was wholly alien. Government in our experience was based on the assumption that our job was to indicate what public money we as elected representatives of the people could make available and to spell out in appropriate detail how we wished it to be spent on their behalf. It was by monitoring what the Chief did with our money and, if need be, by refusing to provide it, that we would be able to ensure that the service was what the public wanted. Should the 'account' rendered by an officer prove to be unsatisfactory, it was open to us to insist on some alternative course of action and even to dismiss the officer if necessary. It was on these grounds that our critics based their argument that our powers were fully adequate to our needs and that all that was lacking was the political will to use them.

This was accountability as we had been reared to practise it. As such it was clearly our responsibility to see that it worked and not that of any officer. The Chief had in fact made this very point to us in the seminar we held on taking office. We were, he carefully explained, the fulcrum of the scales in which the needs and desires of the public were weighed against the advice of the professionals and the availability of resources. This apparently innocuous theory was to prove to be absolute dynamite, as we were to discover. For behind the harmless verbiage lurked the explosive word 'control'.

We set off merrily enough, confident that we knew what we wanted to do. On taking the Chair, my first action had been to revive the tradition that at the session immediately following on the elections the majority should present a statement of its policies and priorities for the coming year. In my City Council days these had been occasions of considerable pomp, graced by the presence of the Lord Mayor on a platform decorated with blooms by the Parks and Gardens Department. Though the County Council conducted its affairs on a much more modest scale, I believed that the tradition was a useful one which should be revived. The police were entitled to know what it was that they were to be accountable for and both they and the public had a right to know where we stood and what we were up to.

As a Labour group we had in fact prepared a manifesto for the elections in 1981. From the vantage point of my enhanced status I recollected with some relish the circumstances of its concoction. The Labour Party office at that time was in the premises of a derelict bank with the counters removed but otherwise complete with all the symbols of capitalism; manager's office, Della Robbia decor in pale blue, immensely heavy doors and a vast safe down in the basement. The place was badly lit and perishing cold; we were on at least one occasion reduced to working by candlelight. It seemed a most appropriate setting for the planning of a revolution. And that, I now realise, was precisely what we were attempting to do, though whether it was to be instant or gradual was a battle not yet joined.

Our manifesto set out our general philosophy in regard to the policing of a democratic society. Our aim, we declared, was to ensure that we had a 'truly accountable police force, dedicated to the maintenance of the public peace on the basis of a fundamental respect for the liberty of the individual' (Appendix I). This, we continued, could only be achieved if the public had confidence in the way the police exercised the powers delegated to them. Then we proceeded to spell out what we saw as the most pressing problems for us on Merseyside and what our priorities would be in dealing with them. When I duly presented this to the Committee at our first meeting, the opposition protested that they were taken by surprise but as none of them had ever given thought to preparing a statement of their own, they failed to respond to my invitation to follow our example.

At the time we took this rather light-heartedly as having enabled us to score over the opposition. Experience taught us that its significance went far beyond that. It is the announcement of their target by the responsible majority that sets in motion the entire process of administering a service. Everything hinges on that original declaration of intent; the designing of a programme for the implementation of the policy, the finding and deployment of the necessary resources, and the monitoring and evaulation of the progress subsequently made. We tried to update the manifesto in each succeeding year, well aware that if we were not flexible and sensitive to changes in circumstance it could deteriorate into dogma, but I must admit that we never gave regular revision the central position in our programme which it deserved. It was because in the rush of events we were apt to forget our overall purpose that our activities sometimes seemed to consist of no more than a composite of bits and pieces.

The outbreak of trouble in Toxteth a few weeks later gave us little time to reflect. Even while we struggled to deal with the complex financial consequences such as the payment of compensation for damages, the urgent need to master the intricacies of preparing the budget for the coming year demanded attention. Floundering through the welter of figures placed before us, it was inevitable that our long-standing determination to get officers out of cars and back on the beat meant that anything to do with vehicles attracted our attention. The Chief was unwilling to co-operate in changing this or indeed any other aspect of his budget on the grounds that his original estimates had been based on careful calculation and therefore were not open to revision; if we chose to disregard his advice, that must be our responsibility. The result was a state of chronic stalemate. Argument about vehicles became a tediously recurrent feature of every agenda which developed as time passed the unpleasant overtones of a personal vendetta. Eventually, desperate to make progress, we cut the number of clapped-out cars due for replacement by a figure more or less snatched out of the air. This was, of course, no way to conduct our business; it bore troublesome fruit in that it absorbed far too much of our time and that of the officers without producing any tangible result.

We had little room for manoeuvre. The budget was constructed on the basis of do-as-you-did-last-year plus whatever extra money could be made available. Given the financial restrictions of the day, this meant that the margin of 'free money' for any new projects we might wish to include was infinitesimal. However any suggestion that we could counter this by switching round the sum of money allocated to existing sections provoked instant hostility from the police. Who were we to say that some amounts should be reduced and others increased? On what information were our proposals for change based? Above all, what right had we to interfere in professional matters about which we were wholly ignorant?

Crestfallen, we rapidly came to the conclusion that there was a great deal more to accountability than the annual exercise of approving the budget had led us to suppose. It was painfully obvious that as a committee we were miserably ill-equipped and ill-prepared for anything more arduous than our habitual role as a rubber stamp. We had to admit that the questions put to us by the police, supported by the opposition, were justified. We did lack information on which to base our decisions. We certainly lacked the skills which would enable us to weigh up the conflicting claims made upon us in our capacity as fulcrum. What we should be concerned about was not, as we had supposed, the efficiency of the Force but that of our own Committee. 'Efficiency begins at home' was the advice of our Treasurer.

We set to work on the task of overhauling the machinery for the administration of our affairs with all the zeal of students who have acquired their first 'old banger'. As we stripped the engine down to its component parts it became apparent that what we had inherited was the wreck of a Rolls Royce. Some bits looked as if they had rusted beyond recovery. Additional parts were certainly required. What we had to determine was whether, if we gave our minds to it, it could be made to serve our purpose or whether there was nothing for it but to scrap the whole thing and go for fresh legislation. Academics debated the issue but for us there was no other option than to make the best of what we had and it was to this that we turned our attention.

The obvious priority was to make sure that we were ourselves properly organised to deal with our responsibilities. Previously all the business had been funnelled into a single meeting of the Authority on a six-week cycle. This resulted in an enormously cumbersome agenda which it was impossible to discuss in any detail. I used to find myself paying more attention to the clock than to the business we were discussing. (It was said that we had to finish our meetings before four o'clock because magistrates with OAP bus passes were not able to use them after that time.) One of our first moves was therefore to set up a Finance Sub-committee, something which should have been done years ago in view of the size of the budget; we topped the million pound mark in 1983. This was resisted by the Chief who, for obvious reasons, was content with things as they were. A rather childish game of shuttle-cock ensued, with items put straight on the main agenda by the Chief, only to be referred back by us to the sub-committee for closer examination before reappearing at a subsequent main meeting, a proceeding which could result in months of delay.

The value of the Finance Sub-committee as a means of getting to grips with particular items in greater detail soon made itself evident and we gradually extended the devolution of business from the main committee to cover every aspect of the service. The result was a network of committees and working parties each briefed to review a specific subject, say, community liaison or data control, before ever the matter was fed into the formal committee system. The Chief rarely attended any of these, declaring that he had a Force to run and had no time for 'me and my committees' but we encouraged his representatives to join in the discussion on equal terms. This was in flat contradiction of their hierarchical habit and the shadow of HQ was apt to cloud their freedom of speech. However, by and large it worked and I have even known an officer so far forget his 'proper' place as to move a resolution.

A hidden benefit to which I thought it best not to call attention was that this way of working enabled me to circumvent the growing trend towards taking all decisions at private caucus meetings without the assistance of our professional advisers. Membership was on a voluntary basis which frequently upset the balance of party representation and deprived a pre-meeting caucus of its point. The only time when a caucus was called was before the main Authority meeting. Though I was gratified by the response of members, I must admit that there were unkind allegations that the attendance allowance was the real attraction and one magistrate frequently demanded to be told how much the meetings cost.

Having set our house in order, the prospect before us was nevertheless a singularly forbidding one. How on earth were we, a handful of part-timers, lay people with no particular expertise, to get to grips with the task of checking whether so vast and complex an organisation as that of the police service was adequate and efficient? The actual checking of how money was spent was straightforward enough in so far as it concerned facts and figures. Any deficiency in accounting for the spending of money would quickly be spotted by our administrators, though there were difficulties in that the police accounting system was out of step with that of the County and this gave rise to friction. But when it came to monitoring and evaluating what we got for our money and deciding whether the service was effective as well as efficient, we were at a loss. This was ground where few had previously ventured.

To talk of the Authority as being the fulcrum of a balancing act conjured up a gratifying image of a statue holding up a pair of scales but while Justice might legitimately perform that function blindfold, it was obviously a most unsuitable stance for us to adopt. We would have to have our eyes very wide open indeed if we were to weigh the public demand for more police on the beat, for example, against the Chief's advice as to the respective merits of more officers on wheels. How to balance an increase in the drugs squad against the crying necessity for better training, particularly in race relations? These and a thousand other questions tormented us. This was, of course, no new problem. My many years as a member of education and social services committees had been haunted by the fearsome necessity to make decisions in such circumstances with no more than a hunch to guide us. There had long been talk of social auditing as a skill which should be developed but nothing much had come of it especially so far as the untouchable of policing was concerned.

The Chief argued that every decision must be taken on the merits of the individual case but this left us at the mercy of such chance factors as which Councillors happened to turn up at a particular meeting, what was on the agenda, what bees buzzed in their bonnets and how susceptible they were to the influence of the Chief. What was needed was some much more exact method of monitoring which would take into account not only professional advice but also the availability of resources, variations in public demand and our own comprehension of the overall needs of the community.

Dismayed by the immensity of the task which confronted us, we decided to restrict ourselves to what was within our capacity, picking out individual items and examining them in detail. We hoped that by this means we would arrive at a method which could then be applied right across the board. Fortunately for us, the Chartered Institute of Public Finance and Accountancy (CIPFA), the professional body of public service treasurers and accountants, had recently taken upon itself the task of assembling such statistics about police expenditiure in general as were available. The Chief protested that the figures were invalid because they did not compare like with like but at least they served as 'comparative indicators'. Looking at the returns from all over the country, some curious variations were to be observed which started all sorts of hares. Why did Merseyside have the most expensive Force in the country bar London? Why the best dressed? Why the most heavily-subsidised canteens? At least we now had some clue as to what questions to ask, a difficulty which had previously seemed to be insurmountable.

Having identified which would be our first pilot studies, we were taken aback to find what a job lot of tools was at our disposal. The Chief had often asserted that administratively, the service was in chaos and this we now found to be only too true. The budget was too generalised to give any indication as to what was actually going on. The statistics of rising crime were alarming but were increasingly discredited by us as we came to understand the basis on which they were compiled. The information regularly available to us was ill-organised and often irrelevant. True, the Chief was required by law to present us with an Annual Report. This was a bulky document but it took the form of detailed factual information about the organisation of the Force and served little purpose as an aid to determining the value of the service provided. We tried gathering together a selection of the Annual Reports of Chief Constables but they turned out to be highly individualistic documents, following no common pattern as to what information they contained or how it was presented and consequently quite useless as a basis for comparing the performance of different Forces.

The annual inspection by the HMI proved equally unhelpful, consisting as far as we were concerned of no more than a rather splendid lunch followed by a round of back-slapping speeches. The Authority never saw the Inspector's report nor for that matter did the Chief though doubtless he had ways and means of discovering its contents denied to us. With the support of a well-disposed HMI we won recognition of the right of the Authority to receive a written report although the argument as to whether this should be released to the public rumbles on. We also developed a pattern of more regular meetings with our Inspector and though on occasion the language used at these was plainer than it was pleasant, they served a useful purpose.

We were shocked to realise how very shaky were the foundations on which the financing of the service depended. It was fair enough that grants should be keyed to the size of the establishment but that in turn seemed to be estimated by guess or by God but certainly not on any rational basis. An experienced Chief Constable once divulged to me that the figure finally chosen was the outcome of horse-trading between himself and Home Office officials in which the Authority played no part whatsoever. For Merseyside, little account seemed to be taken of the stresses consequent on the exceptionally high rate of unemployment. Such criteria as existed apparently applied equally to us as to the havens for the elderly on the South Coast. Accountability for the consequences was so elusive as to be non-existent. Contact with our nominal partner, the Home Secretary, who contributed half of our budget and therefore might be thought to have a responsibility for what we did with the money, was largely conducted through officials. The relationship between ourselves, the Home Office and the Department of the Environment from whom grant aid for the local rates derived was a farrago of crossed lines and contradictory policies worthy of a comic opera.

As for what our consumers made of the service we rendered and for which they paid handsomely, we had little idea beyond the fact that huge numbers of them entered complaints for the handling of which inadequate provision was made. Market research was negligible and the excellent work of the Home Office Research Unit seldom percolated through to elected members. When eventually we were able to initiate projects of our own, we were not surprised to find that what the public wanted was not always what was provided.

One overall conclusion emerged. It had been put to us that if we gave our minds to it, our existing powers could be made to serve our purpose, without recourse to fresh legislation. I was myself left in no doubt that although existing legislation certainly called for review, it was equally certain that no number of new Police Acts would be of the faintest use unless there was also a complete overhaul of the 'managerial account-ability' of the service. To this I believe that we made a significant contri-bution. With hindsight I think it fair to claim that we were well on the way to working out guidelines for good practice so far as accountability was concerned. The basic necessity for free access to information, the im-portance of clarity as to the purpose and policy of the Authority, and the need for skilled monitoring of whatever was to be accounted for; all of these we had established as essential to the practice of accountability. We had no right to sit in judgement on the work of the police unless we our-selves were as fully equipped to do so as was humanly possible. If the police were to accept their obligations to us, we must be prepared to re-spond with an equal degree of responsibility.

We tackled all of this as and when we could. Though it was a fascinating experience and absorbingly interesting, it would be tedious to spell out in further detail our search for the improvement of our performance as a committee and for solutions to the practical difficulties we encountered in our efforts to make accountability an effective reality. I look back on our industry with astonishment. Never a dull minute was the maxim of the day. Even the magistrates, who had at first held themselves aloof from our goings-on, began to join in, voluntarily serving on the endless working parties and sub-committees. Thanks largely to the quality of our adminis-trators, the Authority acquired a reputation for fresh thinking about the principles and practice of accountability as the foundation upon which the administration of policing as a public service must depend.

The pity of it was that notwithstanding this proud boast, the dismal fact remained that we had totally failed to crack the nut of our dilemma. How to delegate authority and yet retain responsibility? We could be as ef-ficient as we liked but if our relationship with the Force was such that deadlock invariably ensued, what price accountability? The inescapable conclusion was that though we had exercised our powers to the full, that alone was not enough. We were well on the way to mastering the art of driving our 'old banger' and were in the process of making sure that it was roadworthy. But what use was that if we were flatly refused the right to sit in the driver's seat or even to issue instructions as to where we wished to go? Obviously the mechanical act of driving must be left to one person but surely we must retain the responsibility for deciding in which direction we wished to be taken? Managerial efficiency made no contribution to the resolution of that issue so long as the police retained the power to veto our right to responsibility for what was done in our name. And the taboo on interference with what was operational would render impotent any attempt to break the deadlock by legislation.

Our predicament was brought sharply home to us by such incidents as that of a request for permission for a National Front march to take place through the heartland of Granby. Strong opposition was generated locally on the grounds of political sensitivity. However the Chief insisted that the decision hinged solely on whether he had sufficient resources to contain any possible disturbance. That was a strictly operational matter and therefore for him alone to determine. This attitude did not, of course, constitute a demonstration of impartiality in the eyes of local people and was widely interpreted as evidence of political bias on the part of the police. What particularly troubled us was that the refusal by the police to acknowledge any responsibility for the political implications of their decision created a vacuum so far as calling anyone to account for the political consequences was concerned. If the march took place and provoked a disturbance, the Chief would be responsible for the way in which the Force handled it, but who would answer for the failure to give consideration to the political impact on the community?

Out of the harsh reality of an endless succession of such episodes it began to come clear that the root of the trouble lay in the habitual distinction between operational and political. We had allowed ourselves to be consistently defeated by the claim that practically every aspect of the service was defined as operational and therefore must be guarded against political intrusion. It was a distinction that we began to realise was both false and dangerous. False because it ignored the fact that the two were opposite sides of the same coin, different certainly but totally indivisible. And dangerous because it stood for a denial of the fact that policing is a public service and as such is necessarily a part of the political structure. Its very existence depends on political decision.

It became alarmingly obvious to us that the horns of our dilemma were far sharper than we had ever imagined. What had happened was that, by law, the Authority carried the responsibility for the provision of a Force but because of the embargo on political interference, we were deprived of all right to determine how we were to carry out this obligation. In other words, power and responsibility in our case were totally divorced. We were held accountable for policies and practices over which we had absolutely no control.

Exactly the reverse was true of the police. Though they might deny in the most categorical language that policing had anything to do with politics, this could not eliminate the fact that every single action they ever performed had political consequences. Willy nilly, even while they roundly declared that they were solely concerned with the enforcement of the law, they found themselves under savage attack for consequences for which they refused to accept liability. They exercised power but rejected all attempts to hold them accountable for what they did with it.

How to convey on paper the slow dawn of comprehension on our part that what this added up to was an entirely new understanding of what was meant by accountability? Originally the fuss had seemed to be all about how the Chief could be more effectively hauled over the coals. It was vaguely assumed that we were talking about some kind of encounter between committee members, suspicious that some abuse of power was afoot, and officials, resentful of being subjected to an unwarranted inquisition by ignorant lay people. Consequently we had fallen into a trap of our own making. We had taken it for granted that accountability was an operational activity and therefore the Chief's responsibility, a one-way process whereby he informed us of what he had done but there was no scope for any comeback on our part.

Clearly we had misled ourselves. Each of us must accept that we shared the responsibility for whatever was done by the service as a whole. And if the responsibility was a common one, we must equally hold ourselves jointly accountable to the public whose service was the sole justification for our existence. The contract between us must be based on recognition of this common obligation. We had no option but, like participants in a three-legged race, to work in partnership. There must be an end to demarcation and to the confrontation to which it gives rise. Seen in this light, accountability is a principle, not a cog in the machinery of government. Its purpose is to serve as the foundation of the relationship between ourselves as politicians and the Chief as a professional. To deny the necessity for political accountability is to undermine the very notion of policing by consent.

This, to me logical, reasoning landed us in the deepest of trouble. As I learned to my cost, even to mention politics and police in the same sentence was to provoke cries of outrage. Far from resolving our dilemma, our insistence that there was inescapably a political dimension to all policing sharpened the whole issue of who was in control of what. To talk of politicising the police, which was what our argument implied, was instantly misrepresented as a proposal to submit them to the control of partisan dogmatists. Even some of those who were harsh critics of policing practice shrank from the thought of politicians having any say in the responsibility for the service. Life was made doubly difficult for us by reason of the controversy over the activists on Liverpool City Council. Nevertheless, there was no evading the issue. As the attention of the police was increasingly focused on the problems of public order, so the political implications of policing policies came under ever more critical scrutiny. The claim to autonomy in regard to their operations could no longer be permitted to pass unchallenged. The police must be brought in from the cold of their self-imposed isolation from the society they exist to serve.

7

The Unacceptable Face
of Professionalism

It would be useless to waste time on regrets that we never pursued our intention of asking the County Solicitor for a report on the role and responsibilities of a Chief Constable to match that which he prepared on those of a Police Authority. Many of the troubles we encountered might have been avoided if we had been clear in our own minds what it was that we expected the Chief to be accountable for. For want of that nail the shoe was lost and the assumption went unchallenged that our difficulties only concerned the relationship between a committee and its chief officer. It took the riots to startle us into recognition of the fact that beyond that obvious source of friction lay the much more fundamental difference as to what is the purpose of policing as a public service. What are the police for? The answer was literally there for all to see on the streets of Toxteth though the interpretations put on the riots provoked sharp differences amongst us. However, it was only when, afterwards, we actually came into contact with those who had participated in the disturbances on whatever side that we began to appreciate the less obvious implications of what was taking place in our name by virtue of the powers we ourselves had delegated to the police.

For me, the extent of the differences between us as to the purpose of policing was brought home with particular force at the Annual Meeting of the local Branch Board of the Federation which took place in the autumn following the disturbances. Ill-advisedly in my opinion, they indulged in all the razzmatazz of opening the proceedings to television. This was an unforgettable occasion; for once, the adjective is no cliché. Normally a beer-and-skittles affair to which the Annual Meeting was only a prelude, this time the hall was packed out. I was the chief 'skittle' as representing the Authority. The Chairman of the Branch Board opened the meeting by declaring that the Force had been 'caught cold' on the streets of Liverpool at the beginning of July (*Merseybeat*, the Force's news sheet, November 1981). 'We were ill-prepared, ill-trained and ill-equipped to deal with the unprecedented violence the members met on those nights.' This remarkable admission was repeated by the Chief Constable when his turn came to speak. These comments were clearly not made in any spirit of apology for their unpreparedness. No attempt was made to explain why they found the disturbances 'incomprehensible and unpredictable' in spite of warnings by those of us who had long foreseen that trouble was on the way. Instead, what came across was the confident assertion that the whole terrible experience justified their belief that the inner areas constituted a criminal community which could only be kept under control by the most 'aggressive and positive' policing. Their only regret was that their use of force had not been more adequate to the occasion. This must never be allowed to happen again.

Little attention was paid to my own attempt to reply to their criticisms of the Authority by pointing out that although we had a declining population and a steadily increasing police budget, we had ended up with one of the highest crime rates in the country and some of the worst riots in our history. My ironic conclusion that perhaps we should consider whether fewer police might bring a reduction in crime was unfortunately taken at its face value. Whether bravely or naively I am not sure, I ended by pleading that we must go forward in partnership. 'I am putting to the next Police Committee,' I told them, 'a request for absolutely regular meetings with your Liaison Committee. For myself, I would like to explore the whole territory of officer involvement, right up to full membership of the Committee. I see no reason why you should not have representatives on the Authority . . . What is needed is a totally new contract between police and public which will be based on equal partnership.'

Any response I might have provoked by this conciliatory plea was promptly doused by the rhetoric of the national Chairman of the Federation. 'I believe,' he declared, 'that last July, the real question that had to be decided at Toxteth was "who rules this city? Is it the law and its officers, the police? Or is it the mob? "' This was to be a fight to a finish. There was no room in it for the likes of the Chairman of the Police Authority or the people she represented. 'Only when crime is contained and reduced, when people feel that the streets are once more safe to walk on, can the police indulge in the luxury of public relations exercises,' was his final conclusion.

The unlovely self-portrait thus presented was that of a Force who clearly saw themselves as law enforcement officers, sent in to impose order, physically if need be, on an unruly people of whose behaviour they themselves deeply disapproved. It reinforced the picture which the Chief had consistently put to us in successive Annual Reports and which was to be read, between the lines rather than on them, of the lengthy report he submitted to the Scarman Inquiry on events in Toxteth. The facts of the situation were, of course, indisputable. The crime figures for Merseyside were exceptionally high and always had been. Sporadic outbursts of rioting and disorder splatter the pages of local history. The Chief's first reaction on coming to the area in the early 1970s had been to exclaim in astonishment at the prevalence of violence on a scale such as he had never before encountered. To him, the conclusion was obvious; Merseysiders were exceptionally violent people, much given to lawless behaviour. Theirs was the original sin. As he reiterated over and over again, it was for the police to control the ensuing troubles as best they could. This was the purpose of policing. Their job was to enforce the law. The very phrase was indicative of what they saw to be their duty.

In the context of the tradition of violence on Merseyside, that could mean only one thing. Force must be met with force. A violent community must be treated with violence. If at the end of the day, that road led to the Public Order Manual of 1985, with its doctrine of intimidation and control, that would be no fault of theirs. This conclusion, once arrived at — though that implies a more calculated decision than ever was taken — all else followed naturally from it. To be effective the police must be equipped to exert authority and command obedience, by force if necessary. As such, their chief officer must necessarily enjoy the unfettered freedom of an army general. There was no scope in such a structure for any notion of being accountable to those on the receiving end; on the contrary, it authorised the rejection of the obligation so to be. Their duty was to enforce the law and therefore it was to the law that they must be accountable. The necessity to seek the consent of the policed became a remote and theoretical concept.

As for the effect their attitude might have on their relationship with the public, the police could see no problem. The law-abiding need have no fear. If the service provided was inadequate, the fault was entirely due to the lack of manpower and resources and the remedy for that lay in the hands of those who complained. The purpose of the complaints system was not to make sure that officers were called to account for their behaviour but simply to defend the integrity of the Force against what must surely be unjust allegations. The bad-apple-in-the-barrel theory provided satisfactory cover for any unfortunate lapses from grace on the part of individual officers.

Even as we listened to what their representatives had to say, I was well aware that the impression being conveyed was grossly unfair to many members of the Force who were, as individuals, caring and compassionate. But that thought simply served to drive home yet again that it was not the manpower that must be our target but the system. No amount of personal integrity could counteract the fact that policing was dedicated to enforcing the law and not to the service of the people. Individual officers might view the problems of life in the ghetto with sympathy but none expressed any doubt as to what their response should be; people ought to be good and must be made to be so as laid down by law. The possibility that conformity to what I once unforgiveably described as their boy-scout-Sunday-school morality might not be achievable or appropriate in the circumstances of life in an area of high stress was a totally unacceptable proposition.

The contrast between the picture presented by the police and that put to us by the groups of residents and people who worked in Granby could hardly have been more stark. What the police offered was policing by the imposition of control, benevolent at its best perhaps but all too often felt to be oppressive, if not actually malevolent. Of the courage and conviction with which they carried out their brief there could be no doubt but nor could it be denied that to the local community the police appeared in the guise of aliens and intruders. They stood as visible symbols of the widespread social prejudice against all who depart from what was regarded as 'normal', be they single parents, non-whites, law-breakers or simply poor and unemployed. There was no room in their thinking for deviance; the law exists to ensure conformity and they were there to enforce it. To a community that carried an exceptionally high proportion of those who failed to conform, whether by birth, by choice or by ill-fortune, this condemnation by the police was obviously a source of deep hurt. Bitter resentment was expressed against the blundering imposition of values which bore little relevance to the realities of life in an inner city.

The police protested that it was to soften the rigours of the law that every constable was endowed with authority to use his discretion. Their confidence that the high standards of the profession and the efficiency of the complaints system provided adequate safeguards against any abuse of this tremendous power was greeted with the scepticism of much experience to the contrary. There was exasperation at the refusal by the police to consider the proposition that the obligation to ensure justice could possibly take priority over the enforcement of the law. That disorder and crime might be the consequence of the breakdown of law and order and not its cause was a thought they had put to the Force in vain.

A leaden sense of gloom crept over me as the gulf between people and police became ever more real. To ask for the bread of justice and be given the stone tablets of the law had demonstrably been a devastating experience. The people of the inner area who came to meet us made a despairing plea for assurance that, to the police at least, they were not 'forgotten people', that they could rely on them for support in their everlasting struggle against a totally unfair burden of adversity. Opposed to this was a judgmental rejection by the police — those on whom they relied as their last resort in a world where all else had failed them — a rejection which was eventually to give birth to the fearful speculation that the police were not 'on our side' but were actually hostile.

To those of us who stood on the sidelines, it was clear that 'the law' had come to be the be-all and end-all of the Force's existence. When we tried to evaluate the service rendered, we were given figures of the numbers of law-breakers they had succeeded in apprehending. The detection rate was their yardstick. It was to the improvement of their skill in catching criminals that their training and their resources were devoted; this was to be brought home to us when later, during the miners' strike, training in crowd control was given such priority that training in race relations was halted for an entire 12 months. The perfection of their technical skills was clearly their pride and joy and their appetite for more resources in the way of computers was insatiable.

It was obvious that once the gulf between police and policed was established, the police found it difficult to understand the way of life they were so quick to condemn. The dads-appoint-lads system of recruitment and appointment did nothing to correct the bar-room ethos which played a major part in influencing newcomers to the service. The use of force to control the disaffected and the violent seemed to us to be a substitute for a solution, an admission of failure. Certainly the law must be obeyed. Certainly criminals must not go free. But justice must be done. The law was a means to that end and not the end in itself.

The most disturbing consequence of all this was that 'the law' had evidently become a kind of Holy Grail, the safeguarding of which was the prime purpose of policing. The law being sacrosanct, so they too were in turn special and separate, entitled to exemption from accountability to anything or anybody other than the law. Since they defined everything they ever did as being concerned with law enforcement, any intrusion whatsoever must necessarily be regarded as improper interference. This made sense of the otherwise irrational intensity with which we as politicians were excluded from anything to do with the service. Enforcing the law was their exclusive prerogative. Politicians keep out.

Aghast, we realised that what confronted us was the face of a totally unacceptable professionalism, a face clouded by fear and disapproval, all the more forbidding by reason of the unbridled power which it concealed and the arrogance with which it was asserted. It never seemed to occur to them that their confidence in their own superiority might be a fiction of their complacency rather than a fact of life. They acknowledged no obligation to the people to whom they owed their being although a profession can only justify its existence to the extent that it subordinates self-interest to the interests of those it serves. Unless this is so, unless every single aspect of the service — selection and training, deployment of resources, policy-making and conditions of employment, even on occasion the enforcement of the law — are tested against that one overriding obligation, then the service is not a profession but a means of earning a living.

The claim that the British police are the most powerful in the Western world if they chose to exercise their authority suddenly took on a dreadful reality. That choice they were now claiming was theirs to make and theirs alone. Their power was absolute. Against its abuse there was no effective means of redress. There is in this country no charter which sets out the constitutional rights of the individual. The police are charged with the protection of our life and liberty and they had betrayed that trust.

What was our alternative? For too long it had been assumed that there was none. Our manifesto in 1981 had been a first stab at putting into words an ideal that was the opposite of what was generally accepted. Our aim, we stated, was to ensure that we had a truly accountable police force 'dedicated to the maintenance of the public peace on the basis of a fundamental respect for the liberty of the individual'. The job of the police was to maintain the balance between the requirements of the community as a whole and the freedom of the individual. At the time we certainly had little appreciation of the full significance of what we were saying because we lacked the practical experience which would have rooted it in reality. This deficiency the riots had now remedied. The upshot was a conviction that there most surely was an alternative and that it lay in a complete turnabout of what had generally been assumed to be the purpose of policing. Put at its simplest, we wanted the police to be servants of the public on whose consent their effectiveness must depend whereas they regarded themselves as instruments of control, accountable to the law.

Take, by way of illustration, the cliché that policing depends for its success on public support. What was brought home to us by the assortment of people we met was that the exact opposite was the truth. The success of policing depends on the extent to which the police support the public. Consent will only be forthcoming if the service rendered gives satisfaction. It was because people had begun to doubt that the police were either able or willing to support them that confidence had declined so disturbingly in recent years. The reason why the demand for 'visible policing' had become so insistent was because the sight of a bobby on the beat was felt to be tangible evidence that he at least was 'on our side'.

This explained many things that had troubled us. We had always been struck by the fact that we received so many complaints about police behaviour. The reason seemed to be that heavy-footed police, and those who went in for the melodramatics of Starsky and Hutch, profoundly shocked people because what they did was in flat contradiction of what was wanted or expected of them. By conveying the impression that they enjoyed nothing better than a punch-up or exerting their authority in a manner offensive to those subjected to it they were seen as antagonists and aliens. Clearly there was a gap between what the public wanted and what the Force supplied.

The police reaction to our approach was predictable and one which secured considerable public support. Maybe our aims and intentions were such as ought to obtain in a civilised society, but could they be anything more than daydreams in the real world of increasing violence and rising crimes? However rational our arguments, however plausible our theories, surely it was beyond the bounds of common sense to talk of policing by consent in the current climate of unrest, disorder, hooliganism and the ultimate horror of terrorism. This was their trump card. Consent, it was put to us, can only be operative in the context of a reasonably stable society where the rules of the game are agreed and accepted by the majority: it would be unutterable nonsense to talk of seeking the consent of the people while shops were in the process of being looted, houses burnt to the ground and life itself threatened.

Mockery of this kind, of which I have had my fair share, betrayed a total lack of comprehension of what consent involves. What we were talking about was not a one-off instant response to an immediate situation: do you, the public, consent to the use of plastic bullets here and now, in the middle of a riot? On the contrary, such successes as had been achieved in defusing potentially troublesome situations could be directly related to the extent to which individuals on both sides had maintained a meaningful dialogue during the previous months and years. Experience in Toxteth was convincing proof that it is never more vital to ensure the 'consent' of the public than in times of high tension such as we had witnessed in recent years and would undoubtedly face with increasing frequency as social and economic pressures bit more deeply. In the inevitable moments when protection and containment demand physical restraint, it is absolutely essential that not only can the police be confident that they can rely on an understanding and supportive public but, even more important, that the public have equal confidence that the police will reciprocate in good measure. To send the police into a crisis situation on any other basis is to make intolerable demands on them which they cannot possibly meet short of becoming an army of occupation.

How to persuade the police to pick up their political responsibilities as a profession? How to politicise policing so that their awareness of their social obligations was raised above its present low level? Certainly we needed legislation to clarify our respective responsibilities, but what else? In the face of the embattled position adopted by the service associations it would have been folly to hope for any dramatic change of heart if only because of the massive dread of political interference which haunted them. Anxiety on this score was, of course, perfectly proper but the lengths to which it was taken surprised me. The panic reaction against the GLC spilled over into the provincial Forces and though the idea that anyone as confirmed a constitutionalist as myself should be feared as a female version of the Ken Livingstone of the media provoked hilarity amongst my colleagues, the consequences were damaging in the extreme. Even our sensible pursuit of the need to ensure that the public got value for its money was interpreted as a naked bid for power which must surely have originated in Moscow.

All we could hope for was that a slow process of what could be called 'political acupuncture' might prove successful where headlong confrontation was bound to fail. Accordingly we were generous in our support of the efforts of the Force to achieve their comparatively recent ambition to gain recognition as a profession. We found money for improving premises, upgrading training, and so on. As a gesture of recognition of the independent status of the Federation we helped to finance the provision of more than adequate premises in place of their previous office in a police station. The Superintendents' Association made no response to the suggestion that they too should seek more fitting accommodation. We welcomed staff representatives at any meetings or working parties they chose to attend and encouraged them to join in the discussions. In an attempt to break down the hierarchical habits which made it difficult for officers to speak out of turn in the presence of senior staff, I secured permission from the Chief to meet staff representatives without his being there but they never took advantage of this concession.

A hopeful development seemed to lie in the Joint Liaison Committee on which the Authority and the staff associations were all represented. Their meetings tended to be occasions for the airing of grievances by the officer side. I did my best to divert them to the discussion of common problems but this received a poor response. Even my request for regular meetings was denied. On one occasion the proceedings deteriorated into something not far short of a kangaroo court in spite of the presence of the Chief. They collapsed into farce when I pointed out that I had not been given a copy of the 'indictment' on the basis of which they were arraigning me. No spare copy was available. The Federation representatives blithely told me that they came specifically to create trouble for me as a means of ensuring their own re-election but I wearied of being an Aunt Sally.

Our protestations that we believed that the future lay in partnership were received with a prickly defensiveness which proved hard to overcome. The most tentative of suggestions that we might be involved in the selection process, perhaps only as observers, were firmly rebuffed and it was made plain that the content of the training courses, even when they concerned local issues and attitudes, was strictly a matter for professionals. Believing that many of the complaints made against officers could be more satisfactorily handled by informal means, we devised various alternatives to the official system but these were invariably opposed. It became a joke amongst us that whenever a proposal was brought before a meeting, the first comment would come from the Federation representative, saying, 'We oppose'. I tried to persuade them that they would disarm their critics if they themselves took the lead in proposing reforms but the more urgently we proferred opportunities for co-operation, the more determinedly they withdrew into the seclusion of their profession.

It became depressingly obvious that we were only tinkering with a problem which affected the entire service, nationally as well as locally. There was little we could do to remedy this beyond supporting the AMA in urging that it was a contradiction in terms that ACPO should claim to speak as an independent professional body whilst they remained snugly ensconced in Scotland Yard, largely at the expense of a public denied any means of access to them and to whom they refused to be accountable. Whether the various associations should be free to join the trade union movement is a separate issue. What matters is that they shall be seen to be independent watchdogs of the integrity of their profession. However ACPO proved to be singularly resistant to change.

Nevertheless I remained convinced that the way forward lay in heightening the awareness of professionalism rather than opposing it. To enhance their pride in the job would work wonders for the morale of the Force, which was dangerously low and ebbing daily. Instead of resenting political intervention in their affairs they must be persuaded to counter-attack by demanding a greater share in the responsibilities of political decision-making. Some of my colleagues were appalled that I should even contemplate such an idea let alone encourage it. They were, of course, right to be anxious: the dangers of rampant professionalism are everywhere for all to see. If the Force actually assumed their responsibilities as a profession, and if they were allowed to make a significant contribution to the governance of the service, they would be in an even more powerful position than that they already occupy.

I shared their apprehension but not their belief that the remedy lay in trying to exclude the police from responsibility whenever possible. Our only sure defence against the abuse of power lay in ensuring that those to whom authority was delegated were effectively called to account. If the professionals were too powerful it was because we as politicians were too weak: it was here that the fault lay and it was this imbalance that must be corrected. With considerable apprehension as to how my ideas would be received by either the Force or my colleagues, I concluded that the onus for taking action rested on us as the Authority. It was our responsibility to see that the system worked to good effect. As the Chief himself had taught us, the Authority was the fulcrum where a balance must be struck between conflicting interests.

I found myself turning the tables on the allegation that politicians were seeking to intrude into the territory of the professionals. On the contrary, it was we who were the injured party, we who were deprived of our right to responsibility. The nettle of political interference would have to be grasped.

8

The Bogy of
Political Interference

Right from the start when in 1974 the new Metropolitan Police Authorities had come into being, our steps were dogged by the bogy of political interference. It was for this reason that our mere existence was so determinedly deprecated. The fact that the Police Authority was appointed by law as the body specifically responsible for ensuring the provision of an 'adequate and efficient Force' was consistently ignored. To whom the Authority as distinct from the Chief Constable should be accountable and what we were to be accountable for were questions which it never seemed to occur to anybody to ask. The relationship between the Authority and its chief officer, and between them both and the County Council, which would have to provide half the necessary money, was simply never discussed. No Home Office guidance was available as to our relationship with either themselves or the Department of the Environment, although half our funding came from central government. If we as Councillors dared to show our heads above the ground, this was promptly condemned as political interference.

My appointment as Chairman of the Authority in 1981 must therefore have been something to which the Force found it hard to adjust. To be expected to work with an elected member who was not only long past their statutory retiring age, who represented an area which they regarded as being occupied by a criminal community, and who in addition to all that was an intellectual and a woman, was wholly outside their experience and foreign to their hierarchical system. It simply could not happen in the police service. My track record as a member of the Police Committee so far must certainly have fed their rising apprehension of the dangers of political interference. I had clearly no intention of being an ornament on the Chief Constable's mantelpiece. It was precisely this which filled them with foreboding.

The County Council had until then operated in the traditional style with committees that in general merely responded to business brought before them by the officers. We were quite content that this should be so. Many of my colleagues in all parties were, like myself, elder statesmen who had shared the general view that election to the County Council was a first step towards retirement. It would have been out of character for most of us to embark on anything that smacked of meddling with the sanctity of the law, especially when it was backed by the intimidating concentration of power in the hands of the Chief Constable.

The influx of newly-elected Labour Councillors in May 1981 changed all that. As the majority party on the County Council, our aim was to become a recognisably Socialist administration. Though I failed to foresee it at the time, the consequence was that the Police Authority meetings became a forum where the forces of change battled it out with established tradition. This was to be a struggle between contradictory ideas but its outcome was to have immediate and practical consequences. I acquired an understanding of what was at the back of all the turmoil only as time passed. It was an experience which on occasion brought the business of the committee to a standstill.

A fair proportion of the newcomers had never served as Councillors before. They had everything to learn; some were aware of their deficiencies, others were not. Lack of experience was something which time might have been expected to remedy. What really constituted the spanner in the works was the legal requirement that one third of the membership of 30 had to consist of magistrates nominated by the five local Benches. This threw the customary system for the allocation of places on the basis of party representation right out of gear. If the party in power was to have any hope of putting its policies into practice it was essential that it should be able to rely on a majority of votes. To the Labour Party that meant that we must take sufficient places to outnumber the opposition plus the magistrates whom we assumed with some justification to be Conservative supporters. The Tories could afford to·be more generous though they too guarded their position with care. Accordingly, when I became Chairman, the Committee consisted of 16 Labour members, 3 Tory and 1 Liberal plus the 10 magistrates, a totally unworkable and undesirable mix. I felt at times like the driver of a bus with four wheels of different sizes plus a brake which was more or less permanently on. No wonder our course was sometimes erratic.

I had learned from our own spell in opposition what burdens are imposed on the minority if their numbers are too low, if for no other reason than that the committee grows weary of hearing the same few voices over and over again. In my turn I had had to endure the painful experience of loud Tory groans and cries of 'She's off again ... move next business . . .' However once in the Chair I rapidly came to realise that the consequences of having no effective opposition have far more deadly effects on the majority. The committee system depends on the minority to ensure that all points of view are properly aired and that the controlling party are made to explain and defend their point of view. In our case this simply did not happen. The tiny Tory opposition was swamped by our superior numbers and the magistrates apparently thought that they were there to adjudicate and seldom made any contribution other than to vote against us. To do them justice, towards the end of our administration they began to take their duties more positively, but their presence was always an awkward anomaly.

The vacuum left by the lack of an effective opposition was promptly filled by some of my own members. Every Chairman has to accept that those who take office automatically begin to look like the establishment and must accept a certain degree of internal opposition. In my case this group, though small in numbers, were bright and highly vocal. Their sharp approach provided a spice to life which would otherwise have been lacking but carried to the extreme to which it was sometimes taken, opposition of this kind could become a threat to the working of the committee.

At first I thought that what we were arguing about was no more than a difference of opinion as to the strategy to be adopted for achieving the goal of policing by consent, which I took for granted to be common to us all. Patiently I plodded away at the task of trying to convince the more impetuous that we had to take account of the fact that public opinion was overwhelmingly against us and pro police, pro plastic bullets and support-ive of the Chief. If we pressed our case too vigorously by demanding the instant dismissal of the Chief and condemning his handling of the riots, we would bring discredit on the party as being against law and order. There was as well the overriding need to get on with the job of restoring some-thing like calm to the streets of Toxteth.

This cut no ice with what I came to think of as 'my activists'. They wanted action and they wanted it now. All of us were weary of the years of wrangling in the Labour Party and the lack of achievement and we shared the same conviction that major changes in policing policy must be made. However it became clear that beneath the conflict over immediate strategy lay a contradiction in our approach to politics so profound that it went right to the purpose of our being. Without appreciating the far-reaching implications of what I was saying, I remarked that the difference between me and my most vocal opponent was that he was in politics to promote the party's policies whereas I was there to serve the people. He was scandalised by the mere suggestion that I should suppose that there could be any choice in the matter; we had been elected on the basis of a manifesto and it would be a betrayal to deviate from it even though only a miniscule number had actually voted for us.

Had I confidence that the manifesto was a genuine reflection of the opinions of the membership, loyalty to the party would have weighed heavily on me. As it was, I was too well aware of the hit and miss process by which the political programme reached the light of day to have any great confidence in it. At one time our practice had been tightly geared to the calendar of the City Council, carefully structured and highly organised. However, the County party came into being with only an impoverished administration to keep it going and a lamentable if understandable lack of support from the grass roots. Consequently the annual conference at which the manifesto was approved had become a fossilised relic of the past, poorly attended and in no way representative of the movement as a whole. It took me some time to realise that there were actually people who took it seriously.

How slow on the uptake I was. Others were quick to seize their chance: the lack of support from the wards provided an easy opportunity for a takeover bid for control by a small group who were united by a common political philosophy. The nature of that philosophy was never spelt out in so many words and indeed its existence was denied by its supporters. The nearest I ever got to a declaration of intent on their part came from a member who told me that he had come on to the Police Committee with little idea as to what it was all about except for his firm conviction that 'control must be in the hands of the Councillors'. Such comments conveyed a fanatical sense of dedication to a dogma. The manifesto was holy writ. As with old-time missionaries to Darkest Africa, there could be no question of seeking the consent of the beneficiaries. It was proof of the unfitness of the common man to play any part in government if he failed to agree.

With what now strikes me as extreme naivety on my part, I ignored the storm signals which began to come my way. It was just not credible to me that the County party who knew little and, I sometimes thought, cared less, about policing should issue instructions to those of us who were actually on the Authority and expect them to be obeyed. There were painful occasions when loyalty to 'the group' conflicted with loyalty to me as Chairman. One incident, for example, concerned the approval of delegates to the Annual Joint Conference of Police Authorities and ACPO. I was taken aback to find that the long-standing tradition that the spokesman for the opposition should be included was roundly opposed on the grounds that as he would not speak for our policies, he could have no contribution to make. This cropped up again later when a more extreme bid was made to exclude the opposition from the meetings of all subcommittees and working groups. On both occasions the day was saved, but only by a hair's breadth.

What finally set the alarm bells ringing was the uneasy suspicion that the party line no longer represented the opinions of the membership but originated in some other source. Who or what constituted this outside influence never became clear but it was increasingly difficult to deny that it existed. Manipulation by Chicago-style bosses has long been characteristic of Liverpool politics but first-hand experience of this new breed who now played a major role in local politics was a revelation. Insidiously the whole drift of policy seemed to change. 'The group' took on an aura of the very sanctity which we so greatly resented in the case of the police. Opposition was regarded as disloyalty. Dogma ruled OK. But it was a dogma to which some of us were not prepared to subscribe.

To those who have never experienced it, the capacity for disruption of applied dogma is hard to comprehend. Why did I not turn and fight my opponents far more vigorously? Partly for the obvious reason that I had no wish to add to the saga of internal dispute that has characterised the Labour Party for too long, and partly because group meetings of serving Councillors tended to be evenly balanced between the activists and the constitutionalists. I had to watch my step carefully because the activists were a more coherent group, reputed to hold their own caucus in a nearby pub prior to party meetings. The traditionalists on the other hand wearied of the endless theorising which caused meetings to drag on into the night and were consequently more often absent than present.

These are explanations that might account for my apparent timidity but the real reasons why my opponents could sometimes sweep the members headlong to disaster lay elsewhere. The simple certainty of the dogmatist was immensely appealing in situations of acute frustration when no way out of the trap of circumstance could be discerned. To beg for patience and moderation at such moments was hard going whereas the confident assertion of the dogmatist offered an escape from the dilemma of which option to choose when all were unacceptable. In any case, it was easier to rouse support for the denunciation of manifest injustice than to plead for loyalty to democratic practice as a way of life.

What is most surely not appreciated is the quite extraordinary difficulty of taking part in a game where one side is committed to playing by the book whereas their opponents acknowledge only one rule, that there shall be no rules. In the Liverpool setting, the thought of a football match conducted on this lunatic basis is beyond imagination yet to those of us who have encountered dogmatism in practice it is an all too familiar reality. The calculated indifference of the activists to the rules of the game dumbfounded me. The end seemed to justify any means. One member actually seemed to think that the findings of the Kinsey survey into crime in Merseyside could be tailored to support our particular policies, a suggestion which Richard Kinsey himself firmly rejected. On one occasion a modest little working party was suddenly declared, in the thick of a meeting, to be a sub-committee with delegated powers; only the professionalism of the Clerk averted disaster. The repeated efforts we made to dislodge the Chief or at least to curb his appetite for autonomy were defeated time and again by the reckless insistence that if the rules obstructed us, the rules were wrong and could therefore be ignored.

I and my kind were, of course, severely handicapped by our willingness to compromise. Our opponents frequently scored over us because to work towards a consensus, which we held to be basic to democratic practice, was evidence of weakness to them. I felt bound to accept the rule of the majority if my protestations of democratic principle were to have any validity but they acknowledged no such obligation. We could never win. If we played by the rules, their freelancing style outsmarted us. If we followed their example, we would have lost before ever we started because we would have sacrificed exactly those principles which we were in business to defend.

Yet each time I yielded a point, I sensed that I had moved an inch further down what could become a very slippery slope indeed. I often wondered whether it was right to continue as Chairman, deeply moved as we all were by the predicament of John Hamilton who, as leader of the Militant-dominated City Council, sought desperately but in vain to maintain some semblance of democratic practice. How to achieve unity and make progress without compromising my principles to the point at which I should have to throw in my hand? I tormented myself with the question, well aware that if I abdicated, my successor to the Chair would almost certainly be someone to whom confrontation would be the breath of life and public satisfaction a fringe benefit. Consequently I found myself forced into some ludicrous decisions which I blushed to put to the committee. Early on, for example, in a fit of pique we abolished the Force news sheet because it dared to criticise us, whilst the saga of the abolition of the police band reached farcical proportions.

Demands for deference to the will of 'the group' gradually assumed what I regarded as ominous proportions. Though accountability was not then the in-word it has since become, this was essentially what the argument was about. If Councillors were to be totally accountable to the County Labour group, then they must automatically be subject to total control by that group. What then of the constituents who put us where we were? Did their mandate run no further than the periodic opportunity to register a vote every few years? The fact that I had been elected as Chairman by the group and not chosen by the leader, as had previously been the custom, took on an unforeseen significance.

It is obvious, seen from across the gulf of abolition, that what we were undergoing was the onset of conviction politics, that is, government where consent extends no further than the delegation of authority to the majority party. This was no Liverpool aberration. Across the entire political front it was becoming increasingly common for those who achieved power by legitimate means to interpret this as a mandate to exercise it without further reference to the wishes of those to whom they owed their position. To apply the adjective Fascist to those who claimed that having won an election endowed them with some kind of divine right to govern was to attract a torrent of pained abuse.

As incident succeeded incident, it became apparent that it was the quickening of the drift towards this new style of politics that injected the note of panic into the police attitude towards us. To them it was as if the bogy of political interference had suddenly stalked onto the stage clad in all the accoutrements of grim reality. When I tried to convince the Chief that however much he might deplore it the new style was a fact of life that we must learn to live with, he roundly declared that he would never acknowledge its existence. Few police officers displayed any comprehension of the dicey nature of my position or of the reasons for the apparent inconsistencies and shifts in policy which were forced upon me by the running fight in which I was engaged. Their insensitivity to the ebb and flow of political life was a constant source of anxiety to me. If they understood so little of the realities of politics, how could they hope to deal with the much more complex relationships within the Granby community? I doubt if they ever grasped the significance of their outright rejection of political control.

I have spelled out the story of the differences with the activists in some detail because, as we ourselves discovered, it is only by close acquaintance that it is possible to grasp the insidious nature of the changes that are taking place in democratic practice today. What was wholly unacceptable about an 'elective dictatorship' was not the strong-mindedness of its leadership, which was in many ways welcome, but the denial of effective accountability which accompanied it. This reduced to futility all the checks and balances which exist to prevent the abuse of delegated authority, as the handling of the miners' strike was in due course to demonstrate with dreadful certainty.

I was struck by the contrast between our own position and that of the Chief in this regard. Within the service, the line of accountability from the constable on the beat right up to the top command was strictly defined. In addition, the Chief was subject to the requirements of membership of a powerful professional body, ACPO, with strong links with the Home Office. Whereas we had a feeble party structure, decaying wards and little effective contact with the national movement. The Authority's links with the County Council were threadlike, our contacts with the Home Office unreal and distant. We operated in isolation; there seemed to be no one who could call us to account for what we did. In theory, the chain of accountability stretched unbroken right from the individual citizen to the Houses of Parliament, but how to ensure that in practice the separate links held firm?

The way out of the quandary came in the improbable guise of liaison with a Conservative Home Secretary. Though technically we were partners in the spending of large sums of money, it had always been customary for the Chief or the Clerk to act as our go-between with the Home Office. The riots startled us out of this habit. By a stroke of good fortune, the Home Secretary at that time was William Whitelaw. His outstanding grasp of how to make the machinery of government work was a revelation.

I met Whitelaw for the first time immediately after the riots when my Deputy and I gate-crashed a buffet lunch at HQ to which we had not been invited. In the few moments of private conversation permitted to us, we raised the issue of our right to responsibility in the light of the Chief's claim to autonomy. Whitelaw listened with his invariable courtesy, his geniality concealing a sense of statesmanship which had previously been absent from our discussions. He took it for granted that we were there to talk politics and from then on made himself easily accessible for that purpose. I regarded the opening up of this line of communication as being of the greatest value though some of my local colleagues thought I would have been better occupied devoting my energies to the campaign to oust our Chief Constable.

I had until this point given little thought to the national scene although on becoming Chairman of our Police Committee I had automatically become a member of the AMA Police Panel. This consisted of the Chairmen of the six 'Big Mets' together with a representative of the City of London Police Committee to which we eventually added a courtesy co-optee from the GLC Police Committee. Shrewdly, given the rising concern about crime and policing, Whitelaw proved to be more than willing to meet us, either as individual Chairmen or as a group under the AMA banner. This coincided with, if it did not actually provoke the development of, a much more positive stance on the part of ACPO. Indeed, I sometimes wondered if we were pawns in some private battle between Civil Servants and Chief Constables although no trace of this was ever allowed to break through the surface gentility of our proceedings.

Perhaps for that reason, or perhaps because we exasperated our civil service colleagues with our constant cry of 'You wouldn't get away with that in local government,' the Home Office set up early in 1983 an unusually small group which became known as the Tripartite Working Party. This was briefed to iron out the recurrent quarrels over management as between the Local Authorities, ACPO and the Home Office. It was chaired by no less than Robert Andrew, the Deputy Under-Secretary of the Home Office, and consisted simply of two members each from the AMA, the ACC and ACPO. I was gratified to find myself involved as an AMA representative in what seemed to me to be affairs of state. The Chief came on behalf of ACPO, I think in his capacity as President Elect. Custom suggested that we were there in an advisory capacity though who we were to advise was not raised at this point. The Federation protested against their exclusion but their freelancing politicising had not endeared them to the management side.

The Working Party's first step was to ask the Home Office officials for some indication as to our respective responsibilities. They forthwith produced a draft of what eventually became Circular 114 (Appendix II). This was presented as being simply for the guidance of Chief Constables on how improved management might enable them to deal with the increasing demands made on their Forces by the constraints on public expenditure imposed by central government. However, we from the AMA having done our homework, meticulously corrected every reference to the Chief Constable so that it included the Police Authority, each taking alternate precedence over the other. We also asked that a paragraph be inserted which would spell out the importance and nature of the role of an Authority in formulating and reviewing the objectives and priorities within which a Force operates, stressing their joint responsibility with the Chief Constable for ensuring that police policies were understood and accepted by the public. In the light of the legislation, these amendments were unexceptionable and they were duly incorporated in the final version.

Our intention had been simply to assert our existence but almost incidentally what resulted constituted a declaration of the essentially tripartite nature of the governance of the police service. Circular 114 for the first time gave practical expression to the belief that policing must be based on the sharing of responsibility by each of the three partners involved: the state, the police, and the people through their elected representatives. It represented a shift in the balance of power between three groups with differing responsibilities but a common purpose, a shift which would make it possible for each to work in harmony with the others without any loss of their own specific sovereignty. Moreover the simple insertion of 'the Authority' in tandem with 'the Chief Constable' had set a boundary to the autonomy of the police, discreetly wrapped up in the guise of guidance but constituting writing on the wall for all to see and clearly understood so to be. The subsequent discreditable denigration of it by both ACPO and the Federation has done nothing to undermine the validity of the principles which it laid down.

Too late, ACPO woke up to the significance of what had been done.

The Chief urged upon me the necessity for us always to get together before meetings in future, a suggestion I would happily have accepted had it been repeated. It was fascinating to observe how the penny of 'tripartite', once inserted, set off a chain reaction right through the system, gathering momentum as it went. If ever there was a case of the right idea coming at the right moment in the right place, this was it. It offered a way out of a tedious stalemate and was welcome for that reason. The local government representatives were assiduous in pressing home their advantage and the word 'tripartite' rapidly became almost a cliché. Almost but not quite. It was surely no coincidence that at that point Whitelaw was removed from the Home Office, to be replaced by a very different sort of Tory. Progressive thinking was out and so was 'dear Willie'. And so in due course were we ourselves.

9
End of Story?

As our life as an Authority drew to a close, all that we had struggled to bring into being disintegrated about us like sandcastles before an advancing tide. The story of our last year or so in office is one long catalogue of defeat. The sweeping thrust of conviction politics and the dastardly attack on democratic practice which it concealed secured victory after victory for 'Them' over 'Us'. The terrifying gap between government and governed which the riots had revealed and which it had been our prime task to bridge, yawned even wider than before; inevitably, nowhere more so than in regard to policing.

United by our common despondency, my colleagues and I watched while the march of events on the national stage confirmed our increasing apprehension. The takeover of political power by the police as a profession continued unabated. The drift towards the setting up of a national Force by the development of Regional Crime Squads continued without reference to the need for a matching increase in their accountability. The slide of the National Reporting Centre into permanence as a non-accountable executive arm of government proceeded without a hitch. The secretly-prepared Public Order Manual, which altered the whole character of policing practice in this country, was brought into operation without more ado, its tactics so evidently based on experience overseas and in Ulster that Granby was talked of as the first of Mrs Thatcher's New Urban Colonies. The arrangements for the Joint Boards which were to replace the Metropolitan Police Authorities confirmed our expectations that they would be no more than toothless jennies. Rumour had it that this was deliberately planned towards centralising the Force. If nationalisation comes, we glumly speculated, could privatisation be far behind?

As the police gained ground we lost it. Whitelaw's departure caused a gale of change to blow down our corridors as his successors rapidly reversed the direction in which we had been moving. The Chief openly repudiated the concept of tripartite government as no more than mere philosophy, his strongest term of opprobrium. A leading ACPO representative publicly denounced 'the infamous Circular 114'. Having set up a working party to implement the recommendations of the Circular, we were undone to discover that the Chief had already prepared his own statement in which the Authority was relegated to a humble position half-way down a list of advisory bodies. We were dumbfounded to be told, on consulting the Home Office, that although we could expect to be consulted, policing policy was the responsibility of the Chief and the Chief alone.

The onset of the miners' strike in 1984 provoked a plethora of argument on all manner of issues but the eye of the storm was indisputably the question of accountability. Never before had the confusion as to who was responsible for what and to whom been more painfully exposed. We who by law were responsible for the provision of the service found ourselves excluded even from information as to the part being played by our own Force. Leon Brittan denied that, as Home Secretary, he had any responsibility for what was happening at the pits since each Force was under the command of its own Chief Constable. Our own Chief, however, declared that his obligations to the National Reporting Centre took precedence over that to his Authority. As for the NRC, the Home Secretary blandly assured us that this was something for which he had no responsibility: if ACPO chose to set up what was regarded by many as an embryo national Force, that was entirely up to them.

So the buck fell down dead at the feet of the individual Chief Constables. There was literally no way in which they could be called to account for their handling of what constituted a national crisis. This was brought home to us with dreadful certainty when, after weeks of pestering, the AMA Police Panel were at last granted an interview with the Home Secretary. The Chief had publicly advised us that by putting the entire Force on stand-by during the first weeks of the strike, he had spent £5m for which there was no provision in the budget and for which committee approval had not been sought. He was, he declared, heading us towards bankruptcy. With total incredulity, we received the Home Secretary's assurance that 'a Chief Constable acting reasonably cannot be required to obtain Police Authority approval for the expenditure involved'. As an afterthought he added that a responsible Chief Constable and his Authority would meet to discuss the situation thereafter. We were too flabbergasted to pursue the matter of who was to decide whether a Chief's actions had been reasonable.

By this single act on the part of the Home Secretary the entire system of police accountability was catastrophically short-circuited. Control over the money had always been the major instrument whereby we, as representatives of the people, could realistically give or withhold consent to the delegation of power to the Force. The denial of our right to that responsibility was, in our opinion, as savage an attack on the fabric of our political system as anything done to our buildings by the rioters. In an endeavour at least to protect ourselves against the Chief spending any more money which we did not have, we explored the possibility of going to the Courts for help but were so disheartened by the legal advice we received that we abandoned the attempt.

Fortuitously, one last stand was made by the County Council, and with some success. In 1985, the Labour group decided that central government controls over local expenditure necessitated an entirely new budgetary system. Traditionally, a ceiling was fixed which must not be exceeded, a process which encouraged officers to make sure that they spent every penny of their allocation. Instead of this, a system was instituted which required officers to start from the absolute minimum of what was already committed and to build up from there. Every single item from the appointment of part-time cleaners upwards had to be separately justified before expenditure could be approved. The Chief was quick to realise the implications of this move. Sooner than yield to what he evidently saw as a dangerous incursion into his autonomy, he preferred to abstain from seeking approval whenever possible.

Meanwhile, incidents of disorder became increasingly frequent on the streets of Granby. Seen from street level, Scarman's philosophy of sensitive policing was interpreted as meaning that Granby was a no-go area where police feared to venture and villains could take refuge with impunity. The Chief was threatened with legal action by an irate jeweller who believed that the chase after his stolen car had been wrongly abandoned when it entered the area. Officers on the beat protested that they were baffled by the ambiguity of their position. The ACLOs found themselves treated as spies and their collection of information to be fed into the planned policing process as a sinister means of control.

The stress of life in a deprived area was given a new dimension by a rising sense of claustrophobia. To those of the Black community who lived there, the walls of the ghetto were felt to be closing in. With the continuing rise in unemployment, fewer and fewer had any cause to move outside that limited area; young Blacks do not often go to football matches. Such as could be identified by the colour of their skin ceased to venture into town lest they be turned back by the police and told to go back 'where they belonged'. Curry was no longer the flavour of the month, an officer was reputed to have said. A fearsome confrontation with the Militant City Council over the appointment on political grounds of an unwelcome candidate as Race Relations Officer briefly united the splinter groups amongst the ethnic minorities as never before.

In the Spring of 1985, in an effort to prevent the escalation of trouble, my Deputy accepted an invitation for members of the committee, accompanied by the Clerk to the Authority, to meet some of the local community. At their insistence, the police were excluded. In the course of these meetings, reference was made by a resident to the possibility that recourse might be had to the use of guns. We were astonished to be informed by the Chief that by taking part in these conversations we and certain members of the staff had behaved in a manner which might be interpreted as being subversive and that an inquiry had been instituted. I was the only Councillor to have been interviewed by an officer at that stage and I consequently acquired something of the aura of a folk hero locally.

As the hope we had cherished gradually crumbled, the resort to violence as a realistic alternative to community policing loomed ever larger. Implacably, each incident gave rise to the next in an apparently unstoppable march to disaster. Each in turn triggered off yet further confrontation. The flashpoint came in October 1985, when a small crowd went down to Court to demonstrate against proceedings being taken against some of their number who had been caught up in the sequence of incidents. They were met by a heavy police presence. Violence broke out as the crowd made their way back to Toxteth. The cars of homegoing commuters were burned. The police reacted with exceptional speed and massive strength, applying tactics for the control and dispersal of potential troublemakers such as had never been seen on the streets before. The trouble was contained. The Public Order Manual was vindicated, but at a cost to the relationship with the public which constituted a major setback.

Confusion mixed with alarm broke out on all sides. The Chief declared publicly his firm intention to maintain order. If the community failed to cooperate more fully in future, he would withdraw the Toxteth Section; sensitive policing was a privilege and not a right. Local people were baffled by the implied reprimand. They valued the beat police. They longed for firm policing. It was left to my Deputy to arrange for two meetings to be held in Granby at which the public might be given a hearing. There was generous appreciation of the prompt action taken by the police in dealing with the burning cars but universal disapproval of the tactics subsequently adopted to prevent further disorder. It was alleged that the use of police vans to clear people off the pavements both at the time of the trouble and again the next day had resulted in a display of violence by the police, of hassle-by-vehicle and racial abuse which was condemned as provocative and unnecessary. It was regarded as particularly undesirable that the Archbishop and the Bishop, present as mediators, should have been subjected to rough treatment.

What emerged overall was the desperation of a community trapped in a rising tide of fear and violence from which it was believed that the police could rescue them if only they chose to do so. It was at these meetings that I heard for the first time public expression of the fear that the dream of the British bobby, to which they had clung so loyally for so long, had failed them. Mothers in the audience declared that they could no longer teach their children that a policeman was their best friend. Their protestations of support for the beat police took on the character of pleas for help rather than assertions of confidence in them. There was in all this no trace of the reaction of a criminal community which resents the mere fact of a police presence in their midst.

In such circumstances it was remarkable that the recurrent outbreaks of disorder were even contained. It was generally agreed that but for the liaison maintained between individual officers and certain residents, the mini-riots of October 1985 might well have rivalled those in Tottenham at that same time. Credit for this must go to all concerned, both police and public, who had quietly gone about the business of building bridges although fearful of taking any open stand which might attract attention. In so far as this reflected the growing experience of the rising generation of British Blacks, it was to be welcomed, but there were those who recognised that if the desire for responsibility which it represented was denied expression, the consequences would be far reaching.

Some of my members saw the remaining few months of our stint in office as their last chance to secure the public humiliation of the Chief and his eventual removal. This seemed to me hopelessly unrealistic but I found it impossible to resist the demand that we should make one last attempt to secure his resignation. Inevitably, this failed. Soured by the betrayal of the fundamental principle of accountability which we had worked so hard to promote, we retreated into acrimony. Relations with the Chief went from bad to worse. Increasingly he went his own way, openly asserting his autonomy when he was challenged as to his disappearance to America for an unspecified purpose which entailed his absence from a vital Authority meeting.

Various attempts were made to remove me from the Chair but it was difficult for my colleagues to dislodge me unless I agreed, which I was not willing to do. It was only towards the very end when the stress of imminent abolition began to bite deep into our morale that things became really difficult. A stroke of smart opportunism resulted in the removal of my sterling Deputy and his replacement by one of those who had consistently opposed me. A proposal for a scorched earth policy before we finally left the scene struck me as so immoral that I feared that I might after all have to resign even at that late date. I struggled to maintain a superficial impression of orderliness at the Authority's meetings but it became increasingly difficult to sustain even that semblance of dignity. When the end came, on April 1, 1986, it was a merciful deliverance.

Is that the end of the story? Obviously not. We on the Police Authority might have been overcome but the people of Granby still live on. To them a battle lost is no more than an all too familiar incident in their lifelong experience of the struggle to survive. The last of the expectations raised by the promises made in the aftermath of the riots have been exposed for what they are worth. The tantalising hope that things might change has been dashed before ever it could turn into a conviction that they would do so. 'They Haven't Done Nothing'. So be it; but life must go on. There is no alternative but to make the best of a bad job.

Yet change there has certainly been, even though it takes on an unexpected form. Seen in retrospect, the mini-riot in October 1985 marked the dawn of a new realism on the part of local people. There is a resigned acceptance of the fact that law and order have broken down, that crime is a feature of normal living. I recollect with sour amusement the old woman who years ago protested that she would have given the mugger the money if he had asked for it but she found unforgivable the indignity of the way in which he jostled her. No one would be shocked by such behaviour now; the anecdote has the air of a period piece. Exhibitions of violence on and off the TV screen are endured with a tolerance unthinkable in the Granby I used to know.

By mutual if unspoken agreement, police and public each mind their own business. The fury of frustration which fuelled the hostility against the police during the riots has sobered down into an acceptance of the reality of the situation as it is now. A local youth club leader, in reply to a question, remarked, in evident surprise that I should ask, 'The police? We have nothing to do with them now.' A teacher commented that the only time the school sees the police is when there is trouble. Granby is not a no-go area, in the accepted sense at least; the police still walk the streets. But by and large they are seen as irrelevant to daily life. They are a Force with a job to do which is no concern of the local community. 'Scarman' is a forgotten dream. The expectations which the talk of partnership roused have been replaced by a matter-of-fact acceptance of the fact that the role of the police is to control disorder and that otherwise they can offer only minimal assistance.

It is said that the real disciplining of the streets is in the hands of an unspecified mafia. Rumour has it that the international drug trade has found it useful to have a base in a supposedly no-go area. There is talk, not unsubstantiated, of vigilante groups enforcing their law against the intrusion of drug peddlers by their own often violent means. A local Black security firm has set up in business. The fear of crime exceeds the reality. People are hag-ridden by apprehension to such an extent that they impose a voluntary curfew on themselves. In this predicament they are grateful for the response they receive from the Toxteth Section and the ACLOs who assiduously attend meetings and functions, though to what effect is uncertain. The run-of-the-mill constables are still viewed with suspicion; the old ambiguity between 'soft' and 'aggressive' policing still lives on.

With that resignation to what is felt to be the inescapable has come an equivalent fall in the expectations that anybody in authority can or will do anything effective about the needs of the inner areas. The great Garden Festival has been and gone, but little benefit has come to Granby: it is said that only two Blacks were employed on the considerable project for clearing the site. Scores of local lads stand idly by to the discomfiture of the white labourers brought in to undertake major schemes for the replacement of worn-out gas and water mains. The 'Minister for Merseyside' has left Granby prettier, but also poorer. Housing Associations and Corporation alike find it increasingly difficult to persuade applicants to accept tenancies in the area. Granby Street shopkeepers battle for existence against unreasonable odds.

The general belief that no help is on the way found its confirmation in the sweeping victory for Thatcherism in the national elections of 1987. Here was proof positive that government by central control is here to stay and nothing can be done about it. The alienation of 'Them' from 'Us' seems irreversible.

Yet as one door closes, another opens. The youngsters, especially those who are Black, are grown men and women now. They no longer need protection against the police. The message is that they can do it themselves, come what may. Alienation has become their way of life. They are no longer supplicants who crave to enter the vineyard. Hope lies in the evidence of political maturity. It was from both Black and white in Granby that there came the most determined refusal to bow to the dictates of the Militants on the City Council, a stand which put to shame the grumbling acquiescence of the majority in the rest of the city. The local elections of 1987 saw a level of participation by the Black community such as never seen before. It reached its peak in the election of a young locally-born Black woman as my successor in the team of Labour Councillors.

The vigour of the new Black separatism distracts attention from the fact that there is also evidence amongst the community at large of a growing impatience with the irrelevance of government. Whereas in 1981 there was a willingness to give 'me and my kind' a chance to 'do it our way', as it was put to me, now people are opting out, going away, taking it upon themselves to manage their own affairs as best they can. The continuing takeover of responsibility for local government by central agencies strengthens the resolve to waste no more time on 'Them'.

This is fertile ground for the seeds of hope for the future of this dogged community of survivors but it is a matter for speculation whether the crop they bear will be one of corn or thistles. The mills of Thatcherism grind remorselessly on with calculated indifference to the lessons of past experience or the potential of the future. In this disintegrated society, there is little chance of success for the blanket solutions imposed by central government. The police respond to what is effectively a declaration of 'UDI' by building up their resources and their skills for the containment of possible disorder. There is little evidence of that 'faith in the city' which is essential if its people are to be set free to make that contribution to the resolution of the urban crisis of which they alone are capable.

Part III

10
The Accountable Society

At this point I must stand and declare myself. I can no longer take shelter behind the generic 'we' I have used so often when talking of the doings of the Police Authority. Not that we ever presented a coherent or united point of view and there are many in my own party as well as outside it who will want to dissociate themselves from the interpretation I have placed on events. So far, I have thought it fair to talk inclusively nevertheless because ours was a common endeavour to which we all contributed even though by opposition. I no longer have that ground on which to stand.

Nor can I continue to claim to speak for the people of Granby by virtue of being their elected representative. The process whereby I achieved that office could not be described as anything more than the most rudimentary of democratic practice but I have always hoped that my commitment to putting myself at the service of the voters in Granby legitimised my claim to speak on their behalf.

All that has gone. From now on, I am out on my own, thrown back on my own resources to make what sense I can of the experiences that have come my way. Is there life after Simey, as a local debating society put it? This book is my own answer to the question, my own interpretation, my own testament. Such merit as it possesses lies in precisely that fact. What I have to say is not the product of intellectual theorising or liberal sentiment about the 'darling poor'. It is not a statement of political dogma. Nor is it a parroting of moral precepts, apt though they may be. What I offer are the conclusions which the brute force of experience has driven me to accept. Nothing nobler than plain common sense dictates that there is no realistic alternative to the way forward that they indicate if we are to remain loyal to the ideal of government by consent. At the same time I must emphasise that unlike the petty dictators of the day, I make no claim that the certainty of my convictions gives me any right to impose them on others. The ultimate essence of democracy is that each and every one of us shall have the opportunity to exercise our social responsibilities and the freedom to choose whether or not to take up that option.

The sudden release from the treadmill of the committee cycle and the narrow commitment to policing which followed on the abolition of the County Council in April 1986 was a heady experience. Mulling over the piles of paperwork which I had accumulated during the years of my time as Chairman of the Police Authority and such diaries and notes as I had kept, I at first despaired of attempting to reduce to order the welter of material at my disposal. But as I regained something like detachment from those five years of the most intensive labour I had ever undertaken, I looked at the world about me with fresh comprehension, only to discover that what had at the time seemed to be a unique journey of exploration was, in fact, the common experience of our times.

With a sense of revelation it gradually became apparent to me that for all its variety, the story I have tried to tell is dominated by a single theme. And, moreover, that the theme is a universal one which goes far beyond either Toxteth or the police. No one, not even the most obdurate of Chief Constables, ever dared to deny the principle that policing in a democracy must be by consent. What had given rise to conflict was the question of how to put that principle into practice. In other words, it was the political process of governing the service that proved to be our real stumbling block regardless of the nature of the immediate issue at stake and quite apart from the pros and cons of any particular strategy or policy. How were decisions to be reached, by whom, on what basis, and above all, for what purpose? Which of us was accountable for what and to whom? That was the rock on which we foundered so repeatedly and so disastrously.

Like a tap on the elbow of a child peering into a kaleidoscope, this shift in my point of view changed the whole pattern of my thinking. With astonishment I realised the existence of a gap a mile wide between what we thought we were doing and what I now discerned as having been the true object of our activity. The pieces were the same but the picture was entirely different. The truth was that we had been so absorbed in the hurly-burly of the daily argument that we had completely failed to grasp what the conflict was all about. It was now plain as a pike-staff that the focus of our concern had never simply been the police as such. Changes in police practice were a by-product, not our central target. We had thought that our problem was that of reforming the operation of the Force when what we were really worrying on at was the issue of the relationship between ourselves as politicians and the Chief as a professional. There could, of course, have been none better to serve that purpose than policing because of all the public services it is the one which carries the fundamental responsibility for the relationship between the state and the individual citizen. If we get that relationship right we need have no fears about that between government and governed.

The effect of that simple shift in perspective was to reduce the confusion and conflict of the previous years to a pattern and a coherence whose existence I had never suspected. I found myself reinterpreting every

last thing we had ever done. Incidents which had borne no apparent relevance to the mainstream of the debate acquired an unexpected significance. What had seemed at the time to be insurmountable obstacles shrank
into mole-hills. The true target of our endeavour came out sharp and clear
like a mountain whose summit is revealed by the parting of the clouds.

With the benefit of my new insight, it was easy to see where we had
gone astray. When we took office in 1981, we had started out with the
glib conviction that all we had to do was simply to make the Chief more
accountable. The Kelly case, the 'Great Budget Row' and then the riots
had all pointed to that single conclusion. The trouble was that all we had
by way of guidance was the well-established assumption that accountability was some kind of executive tool designed for the specific purpose
of enabling a committee to control its chief officer. To us the purpose of
accountability was quite blatantly to assert the fact that 'we are in control
now', as some of my members did not hesitate to declare publicly.

It was an ambition we never abandoned right to the bitter end. Yet curiously, reading the records all over again, it is as if all the in-fighting was no
more than a ruffling of the surface while deep down below the tide was running strongly in a direction which was the exact opposite of our intention.
In practice, all our rhetoric about political control amounted to precious
little. Try as we would, our bids for power usually ended up with the reverse outcome; the Chief firmly in control and we elected members left
carrying the can of accounting to the public for what he did. It was simply
not feasible for lay Councillors to control police operations. Reluctantly
even some of the most radical amongst us began to think the unthinkable
thought that perhaps it must necessarily be so; control has to be absolute
if it is to be effective. Had the National Front march gone ahead, the Chief
would have had to be in charge while it was actually in progress. He had to
be in total control of the policing of the riots while they were actually
happening. There could be no half-measures, no reservations.

Consequently, quite early on we found ourselves faced with the apparently contradictory proposition that it was not for us to run the Force but
to see that it *was* run. This was the first time anything like a job specific-
ation had emerged and it went a long way towards clarifying our role as
distinct from that of the Chief. The implication was that no matter what
operational control was delegated to him, our responsibility was to see
that the service provided was what the people who had elected us wanted
and needed. There was absolutely no possibility of handing that over to
the Chief; it was our specific and particular responsibility. His obligation
was a professional one, ours political, and the two were quite distinct even
though they were inextricably linked.

It was translating into practice what was, to us, a novel distinction that was to absorb so much of our attention throughout our years in office. All the work we did on improving our own efficiency as a committee was directed towards making us more effective as 'auditors' of the 'account' rendered to us by the Chief. How far that was a passive role and how far we were justified in using it as a means of insisting that the Chief should carry out our policies was the bone of contention over which we fought so persistently. Our entire programme for liaison with the community was designed to that same end and here again where we had parted company was over the eventual purpose; was it to enable the people to take responsibility for ensuring that their wishes were carried out or merely to win their support for decisions made by the police? The refusal of the police to acknowledge the right of the people, or of us as their representatives, to political responsibility struck right at the heart of the principle that policing must be by consent. Belatedly I recognised that it was the very issue which underlay my own quarrel with the dogmatists.

The unexpected outcome of our search for control was thus what amounted to a completely new understanding of what we meant by accountability. It was because we had been aiming at the wrong target that we felt that we had failed but in fact, almost by accident, we had hit the bull's eye. From interpreting accountability far too narrowly we had moved forward to the realisation that control is a by-product of accountability and not its real purpose. Accountability is not about control but about responsibility for the way in which control is exercised. The distinction is a fine one but it is of fundamental importance. In other words, accountability is not an administrative tool but a moral principle. Of those to whom responsibility is given, an account of their stewardship shall be required. It is a principle whose purpose is to govern the relationship between those who delegate authority and those who exercise it.

That went for us as much as it did for the Chief. And, we began to think, for those who in turn delegated authority to us and to whom we ourselves must be accountable. They too carried a particular responsibility for the way they played their part, a responsibility which was theirs by right of citizenship and of which they must not be deprived. With a flash of insight, I realised that just as we on the Authority had so bitterly resented what we believed to be the unjust deprivation of our right to responsibility at the hands of the police, so too the people of Toxteth had rebelled against their own deprivation of all that goes to make up self-respect. At last I understood the message which had been so dramatically shouted out to us on those wild nights of the summer of 1981. We had got it all wrong, back to front, upside down, inside out. It was not the police we should have been concerned about but the policed. It was we and not the police who had failed the people of Toxteth. It was not the Chief's accountability that should have worried us but our own. On and on it went. We had asked the wrong questions; no wonder we came up with some funny answers.

It is justice the people of the inner cities cry out for, not 'nice' policemen or more jobs or better houses, not a bigger share in the handouts of an uncaring state. The riots were a demonstration of profound significance. What those we met after the riots tried to tell us was that they were exasperated beyond bearing by their enforced alienation from the rest of society, their allocation to the bottom of the bucket as a 'base community' of the unwanted and the rejected. They were protesting against being trapped in a mechanism of dependency from which there was no means of escape. They protested because they were denied the compassion and support of a caring community to which we are all entitled in times of adversity. It was the denial of their 'right to belong' which lay at the heart of the riots. They were and still are the victims of an apartheid of poverty. The police were the targets of their anger because they acted as agents of the state in enforcing that alienation instead of protecting the people from it.

A far cry, this, from our original simplistic ambition to control the Chief. Eyeing the story which is set out in the previous chapters not as a documentary about policing but as a political case history, it is at once evident that it raises issues of universal concern. The gulf between the police and policed was not something special to the Force but typical of that between government and governed, 'Them' and 'Us'. The virtual takeover of political power by the police was no one-off special scoop on their part but evidence of the malaise which afflicts our entire system for managing our common affairs. It is an indictment of our times that we have allowed the principle of the right to social responsibility, which is or should be a universal attribute of citizenship, to become mere theory. We pursue our rights with an almost hysterical zeal but remain totally indifferent to the complementary duties which justify them. Government by consent implies a responsible society, one in which every individual without exception is able and willing to accept the obligations as well as the privileges of citizenship. In our original manifesto we had declared our aim to be the establishment of a 'truly accountable police force'. To that would have to be added the need for a 'truly accountable society'. To the maxim that there can be no taxation without representation must be added the rider that there can be no representation without accountability.

We ended up in defeat on all fronts. But I remember my Professor at the University who, when surprise was expressed that he should leave Oxford to come to Liverpool, replied that it was as enlightening to study our life and times in decline as in prosperity. I believe that we learned as much by failure and tribulation as we could have done from success. What then has the tale of our years as an Authority to contribute as we venture into the new world of the next century?

One thing is absolutely certain: there can be no going back. Those of us who experienced at first hand the disturbances in Toxteth in 1981 grasp perhaps better than most that, on those nights of wild destruction, an epoch ended. The bulldozers which then moved in cleared away more than rubble and ruins. A way of life had gone. Realistically, we have no option but to go forward. Profound and lasting change is upon us and cannot be evaded. What is called for is no mere repair job designed to restore the past to working order like a steam engine in a museum. The Industrial Revolution has been and gone and with it the way of life to which it gave rise. Any attempt to meet the current urban crisis on the basis of backward glances at defunct Victorian values is a recipe for failure. By all means let us learn from the past but there can be no talk of reverting to the dear departed days of long ago.

What is required is a strategy which will boldly use the past as a spring-board into the future. The life we now contemplate requires a way of managing our common affairs expressly geared to the circumstances of today. Just as the rioters burned and destroyed on a selective basis, so we must sift out from the wreckage what is fundamental to our purpose and challenge the survival of the assumptions and habits of thought which are our inheritance. We must rescue the basic principles from the ruins of the past, like villagers who use the stones of an old castle to build a better way of life for themselves.

How ironic, in view of the saga of head-on confrontation that is the stuff of my story, that the one absolute conviction to emerge from it all should be that government by consent necessarily implies consensus. Our experiences cannot be interpreted in any other way. Squabbling over who should be top dog got us nowhere; as soon as either side scored a victory, the quarrel immediately broke out all over again. Inevitably so, since the dilemma of our relationship with the Chief was an ongoing one which recurred daily and hourly. There never could be a once-and-for-all resolution of it if the principle of consent was to be anything more than the token gesture of casting a vote at rare intervals. Collective government, which is essentially what government by consent is all about, requires that a balance shall be struck between conflicting interests and opinions by agreement. This cannot be achieved by the imposition of a decision by one side on the other. As in riding a bicycle, the striking of a balance depends on complementary pressures being exerted by each side in turn. A balancing act must be based on partnership. Conflict is stimulating and the right to disagree is essential; nobody enjoyed the rough and tumble of argument more than I did myself. But the final decision must not be the bogus consensus which prevails when those in power use that power to impose conformity on others. Ours must be the politics of reconciliation, not confrontation.

Is talk like this mere day-dreaming, an escape into fantasy from the oppressive reality of the contemporary scene? Maybe so, but without a vision the people perish. As our efforts to improve the efficiency of the Authority taught us, the first essential is to be clear as to what is our objective. To cherish a vision is the best corrective of our vulnerability in the face of those who would impose their will upon us.

The stock reply to any such idealistic proposal by those who hold positions of authority is to pay lip service to it but to qualify their support by a cynical disbelief in the capacity or the willingness of the public to respond. They, meaning the people at large, are not ready yet, we are confidently assured. I heard that one right round the West Indies in the run-up to independence. It underlies the philosophy of those who clamber aboard the bandwagon of the inner areas crisis, intent on replacing what remains of local democracy by central controls. The arrogance of this school of thought has always shocked me. The people who are so denigrated have survived circumstances of life far beyond the comprehension of those who sit in judgment on them. Many of those who live in 'communities of endurance' demonstrate an incredible loyalty to the basic decencies of human society. To write them off as unfit to manage their own affairs reveals an assumption of superiority which is a compound of ignorance and selfishness. It is the foundation upon which apartheid is built, be it in South Africa or Granby, Third World or First.

This argument is backed up by the equally cynical assertion that anyhow, nobody nowadays wants responsibility or feels any need for it; all the human race cares about is their own selfish self-preservation. Certainly ours is a society where the level of social awareness is pitifully low. We don't want to be involved. We have been reared to dependency on rules and regulations, benefits and bonuses, and know no other way of life. The takeover of our social duties by a centralised government leaves us cold. The denial of our right to vote by the cancellation of the local elections in 1985 roused remarkably little protest though to me, as a one-time cadet in the suffrage movement, it stood for something not far short of the end of the world. As a society we are simply not aware of the creeping erosion of such right to social responsibility as we ever had. We have no vision of what might be.

To acknowledge that all that is only too dismally true is, however, not to be taken as an admission that to talk of promoting a universal sense of obligation towards our fellow beings is evidence of lunacy. The fact that it is almost impossible to love your neighbour in the Welfare State is not proof that the need to do so does not exist. Indeed what draws so many to live and work in the inner areas and the Third World is that spontaneous altruism flourishes there to an extent unknown in more 'civilised' communities. The truth is that though investment in what passes for participation may be at the point of extinction, the need of the individual to belong to some human grouping lies buried deep beneath the slagheaps of materialism. The need exists all right, but we fail to recognise it. For lack of that vision, the people perish.

There is undoubtedly little enthusiasm for participation as it is commonly practised yet at the same time there is evidence of a positive hunger for the right to recognition as a member of society. Loneliness is another name for it. The widespread disillusion with the Welfare State is a reflection of a deep longing to be part of a caring community, to be a contributor whose presence is valued as well as a recipient of the benefits of membership. The constant lament of the forgotten, the Black, the old, the unemployed is for a place in the vineyard; they crave to be wanted. Poverty is no new experience to them but to be cast out as they are by modern society is an intolerable deprivation. Regrettably, the focus on the urban areas distracts attention from the fact that it is also a deprivation from which we all suffer. There is no scope in our political structure for what Titmuss called 'the gift relationship'. Yet it is as essential to the continuation of any human society as is the necessity to ensure individual survival.

What is called for is quite simply a new emancipation movement which will set the people free from the domination of bureaucratic controls and partisan dictatorship and inspire them to demand a far greater share in the making of decisions of general concern. The need is for more politics, not less. Democracy must be democratised. The times have moved forward but political practice has stood still. Our aim must be to bring about a vast improvement in the level of awareness of social responsibility. Whether it be professionals or politicians, those who govern or those who are governed (and we all fall into different categories at different times), that need is universal. We have failed to adapt to being members of an urban community. As a society, we are hopelessly unprepared for what is required of us. If we are to accomplish the giant leap forward in the practice of government which the post-industrial era demands of us, we must set ourselves as a nation a far higher standard of political skill and understanding than we have ever aspired to before. Our best defence against the creeping acquisition of power by 'Them' is a politically educated people. We apologise because after a hundred years of universal education a minority are still not literate but we are indifferent to the fact that for possibly the majority, the level of 'politeracy' is abysmally low. As a society we are plain dumb ignorant as to what are our rights and duties as citizens or how our common affairs are handled.

Political awareness alone will not be enough. Unless outlets are available for the aspirations thus engendered, the outcome will be yet further explosions of frustration such as we experienced in 1981. Those who are ensconced in the corridors of power must open the doors and let the people in. A whole range of previously unimagined opportunities for sharing political responsibility will need to be devised. The way-out proposition that 'barefoot bobbies' might serve our purpose is only a trailer for what must come.

To these two — advances in political know-how and improved opportunities for the sharing of power — must be added a vigorous political will. It is essential that all three must interlock if an upward spiral of continuous endeavour is to be set in motion. In the past, what prompted political action was the struggle for the universal right to work and the improvement of the conditions of the workers. It was as a worker that the individual could claim the right to enjoy the benefits of citizenship. That imperative is no longer valid and may never be so again. It must be replaced by a new aspiration to create a society which values the individual in social rather than economic terms. The imperative of the future lies in finding some other means of ensuring the universal right of the individual to a place in the society to which he belongs. 'The gift relationship' must become a daily experience for every single person. The nineteenth-century tradition of voluntary service as a perquisite of the leisured must be drastically redefined and enlarged so that it becomes a universal right of citizenship.

Coming down from the delectable heights of cloud-cuckoo land to the flat ground of real life, what hope is there that any or all of this can be achieved? There is no denying the fact that to urge such a case as I have outlined is to fly in the face of the gale-force winds which blow in a totally opposite direction in today's political climate. Certainly there are signs that people are beginning to sicken of a surfeit of materialism. For those to whom comparative comfort is a first-time experience, the satisfaction of acquisition has not wholly destroyed the appetite for a better way of life. Unemployment has forced many to discover that there is more to life than wage-earning. Nevertheless it would be utter folly to pin much hope on changes of this kind in face of the high-powered commercialism by which materialism is constantly nourished.

Where then can we look for help? The grip of Organisation Man on our system of government will not easily be loosened. Custom and habit make it extremely difficult for us to break away from the restrictive traditions of committees with agendas and reports and mountains of paperwork. The professions habitually oppose whatever they see as an intrusion into their private empires; their track record as defenders of their own interests against the people they exist to serve is not impressive. It would be equally forlorn to hope that any lead will come from the political parties, given the present political climate. Deprived by the 'elective dictatorship' of the majority party of any opportunity for effective intervention, the opposition parties disintegrate into fractious argument amongst themselves, a replica of the situation in Granby today. The dogmatists of whatever party have no desire to serve an educated public; conviction politics feed on ignorance and apathy. The deadweight of the bureaucracy of which elected members are necessarily themselves a part defeats all but the most stalwart. Even amongst those who oppose the current trends there is a dismaying acceptance of what is regarded as inescapable.

The many committed workers in the churches and the voluntary agencies are hampered by their loyalty to the values and the attitudes of the past. They talk of bringing their faith to the city but with notable exceptions (and not a few of them in Granby) they have themselves little faith in the people who live there. Neither the system nor often their own inclination offer encouragement to abandon established ways of working in favour of letting people do things their own way and learn by their own mistakes. The remarkable welcome accorded to 'Archie and the Bish', as the two Bishops are popularly known, is an indication of the response which can be evoked by those who come in a true spirit of service.

A glum note on which to end? Adamant as ever in my refusal to bow to the demands of the dogmatists for compulsion as the only way out of our predicament, I find myself turning back yet again to the inner areas to refresh my flagging inspiration. Our best hope, indeed I would almost dare to say our only hope, lies in the company of the oppressed and the alienated. They already cry out for liberation and need no urging. They are of necessity a communitarian society, to use the hideous word which is all that is available to us since both 'socialist' and 'communist' are burdened with partisan connotations. Unlike the prosperous, the sharp pinch of adverse circumstance has never allowed them to forget their common humanity. That in Liverpool they should demonstrate this with the wit and ingenuity which has become their characteristic is a consequence of the pooling of cultural resources of exceptional richness.

It is no coincidence that it was the Black community in Granby who led the revolt against the dictatorship of the Militants on the City Council nor that it is in the inner areas that resentment against the imposition of control by the police rouses the most fierce resentment. It is not by chance that the most impressive of the self-help groups have emerged in the inner cities, driven by necessity to invent their own solutions to the problems which beset them. More often than not they triumph in the face of fierce opposition from the powers that be. Theirs is no criminal community, no dustbin for the discards of a selfish society. These are people whose loyalty to the pursuit of a better way of life has been put to the bitter test of injustice at the hands of their fellow men.

The wheel has turned full circle. I am back where I started. It is in the company of the people of Granby that I have rediscovered democracy, reduced to its bare essentials but a living reality nevertheless. It is they who have redefined altruism for me. To them, to stand by others in their time of stress is no matter of duty or conscience but a realistic demonstration of the fundamental principle that survival depends on mutual aid.

So, for all the heartbreak, the physical fatigue and the draining of the emotions which my long association with Granby has brought me, at the end of the day I am left with the infinite benefaction of a renewed faith in my fellow men and women and a deep affection for them. It is in them that I catch glimpses of the divine. Long may they survive to the benefit of us all and to the greater glory of whatever god presides over the destiny of the inner cities.

Appendix I

Merseyside County Labour Party

A Policing Policy for Merseyside

The aim of the Labour Party's policy is to ensure that we have a truly accountable police force, dedicated to the maintenance of the public peace on the basis of a fundamental respect for the liberty of the individual.

This aim can only be achieved on one condition, that the public have confidence in the manner in which the police exercise the very considerable powers delegated to them. Recent experiences suggest that the increasing size and sophistication of our modern forces are in danger of undermining this principle. The police seem to be increasingly remote from the public, even on occasion, alien to them. While we are committed, therefore, to the provision of a strong and effective police force, we are emphatic that it must be one which is firmly under democratic control and highly sensitive to the feelings and needs of the local community which it exists to serve.

This does not mean that we have any intention of breaching the tradition of the British police, that they must be independent of day-to-day politics and free from misuse by party politicians for their own ends. On the contrary, we will do our utmost to preserve that tradition and to prevent it from being subverted by the creation of powerful police forces which control, rather than are controlled, by the people.

Do We Need More Police?

As Socialists we utterly reject the argument that the only answer to the current anxiety about law and order lies in ever-increasing numbers of police with ever-increasing powers over the freedom of the individual.

On grounds of cost alone, the implications of such a policy are unacceptable. The cost of policing Merseyside for 1980 amounts to an astonishing £67 millions, an actual growth at a time when all manner of other public services are suffering harsh cutbacks. But cost apart, there are fundamental objections to a policy of 'more' as an answer to the needs of our times. We believe that the causes of crime and social unrest lie deeply embedded in the social and economic structure of our society. To rely on increased police activity as the principal means of

127

dealing with the symptoms of social malaise would be to require the police to act as an instrument of oppression.

The Key Role of the Police Authority

Most important of all, a policy of 'more' ignores the urgent necessity for a thorough review of the present system of accountability. It is significant that the legislation giving increased powers to the police in Scotland makes no reference to any equivalent strengthening of democratic control.

The Police Authority (that is, the Police Committee of the County Council), is by law, the body responsible for the provision of an 'adequate and efficient' police force for the area. It is to them, in the first place, that the police are accountable. However, it has become apparent that the powers given to the Authority by the Police Act of 1964 are increasingly inadequate in the circumstances of the 80's. Consequently the police have assumed a growing share of the responsibility for policy making and the Authority has come to be regarded as little more than a rubber stamp. New legislation is clearly required if this undesirable situation is to be corrected. For example, the compulsory inclusion of as many as ten magistrate members, not accountable to anyone, and the restrictions on the consideration by County Council of the police budget, make a mockery of democratic control. We would therefore support initiatives by Jack Straw, and other M.P.s to obtain changes in the law to ensure the greater accountability we seek.

Nevertheless, it must be admitted that legislation alone will not remedy the poor performance of the Police Authority of today. There must be on the part of elected members a new conviction as to the absolute necessity for effective democratic control.

There is no doubt that the really energetic exercise of such powers as the Authority already possesses could do much to restore the balance of power as between police and elected members. In particular the right to ask questions and to require reports, vigorously applied, could become a most valuable means of ensuring that policing is at least subjected to searching democratic scrutiny if not to actual control.

What Do We Propose?

It would, therefore, be Labour Party policy, as a top priority, to initiate a continuing review of whatever issues cause public concern, or create problems for the police. The misgiving with which any kind of 'task force' is regarded is an example. Police Authority meetings would become a forum at which police and elected members would discuss together, in public, ways and means of dealing with the dilemmas and difficulties of policing a modern community. The aim would be to produce an agreed policy, understood by the public and acceptable to them. Consideration would be given to holding the meetings in the evenings, so that both public and the media would be enabled to hear for themselves on what basis decisions are taken.

In so far as the root causes of anti-social behaviour (such as vandalism and violence) call for political decision[s] reaching far beyond the enforcement of the law, we believe that responsibility for action rests squarely with the elected members and not with the police. We would therefore expect the Authority to play a leading part in the promotion by the County Council of a co-ordinated social policy which would draw together all the public services in a common endeavour to alleviate conditions of social and economic stress. To this, the police would, of course, make a vital contribution.

In addition, every opportunity would be sought for members of the Authority to meet the public for an exchange of views as to the 'adequacy and efficiency' of the service provided. After all, it is the elected member and not the Chief Constable who can be dismissed by the dissatisfied customer! Similarly, we would implement the recommendations of the Edmund Davies Report by holding regular meetings with the representatives of the Federation and other ranks. In this way, elected members would gain an understanding of and sympathy with the working conditions of the men and women who constitute the force. Consideration would be given to the question of police membership of the Trade Union movement.

Specific Issues
Complaints
We would support the demand for a more open system of handling complaints, including an independent element. The Authority would be urged to revise its procedures with a view to ensuring a much more intensive scrutiny of the way in which it exercises its responsibilities. This would include an examination of the reasons for complaint with a view to remedying any which are preventable. The way in which the Authority responds to expressions of public concern over particular incidents urgently calls for overhaul. The existing system is geared solely to the maintenance of force discipline, and apportioning individual blame: consumer satisfaction should be given a much higher priority. The involvement of the local member, at local level, in particular, should be considered.

Sus, Stop and Search, etc.
The Authority would initiate a system of monitoring the extent to which various legal powers concerning such offences are used locally, with

special reference to the frequency of complaints of their abuse, both on the streets and inside police stations. We would support the campaign for the repeal of such laws.

Traffic Offences
The rate of prosecution for traffic offences compared with that for cautions is higher than average on Merseyside. Current policy should therefore be re-examined. Regular consultations with the Highways Committee should be sought as to parking, street lighting, road improvements, etc. in so far as they affect policing, and road safety.

Alcoholism, especially amongst young adults, is increasing. The Authority should accept responsibility for policing policy in regard to this situation. Co-ordination of effort as between the Courts, licencees and others, based on a careful analysis of the facts, is urgently required.

Public Order
We would press for the control of street marches, demos, pickets, etc. to remain with the Local Authority, and not removed to central government. A guide to local requirements in regard to such events should be made freely available.

Public Spaces in Flats, Pedestrian Ways, etc.
The problems of policing open areas of this kind give rise to public concern. The Authority should co-operate with other services, such as housing and cleansing, to devise a common policy designed to increase the sense of security.

Computers
The Authority should institute regular checks as to what information is stored, by whom it is collected, for what purpose, and how access to it is controlled. The Home Office should be pressed to set up a Data Protection Board, and to issue guide-lines as to the protection of individual privacy.

Liaison With The Public
We would seek to intensify the programme of in-service briefing in order to assist the force to keep abreast of new legislation and current problems. In particular, there is a need to ensure a more adequate understanding of the issues underlying expressions of social unrest which stem from industrial conflict, political protest and similar causes. The Community Liaison Scheme should be evalued as to the extent to which it is successful in securing support for the police. There should be a two-way flow of information as between police and policed by the use of the media as well as

more local means. The involvement of the public in making provision for school crossings, road safety, crime prevention, etc. should be encouraged.

Race Relations
The existence of racial prejudice, both in the force and in the public in general, calls for a positive programme of efforts to counter-act such attitudes. It is particularly important that the black community should have confidence that liaison is a reality and not a window dressing operation.

August, 1980

Appendix II

Dear Sir,

Home Office Circular No 114/1983

Manpower, Effectiveness and Efficiency in the Police Service

Introduction
The purpose of this circular is to inform Police Authorities and Chief Police Officers of the considerations which the Home Secretary will take into account in carrying out his statutory responsibility for approving police establishments; to invite Chief Officers and Police Authorities to keep their objectives, resources and priorities under review; and to inform Police Authorities and Chief Officers of the relevant matters on which the Home Secretary has asked HM Inspectors of Constabulary to concentrate their attention. It reflects the experience which forces have gained in the development of different policing methods and styles of management, and has been prepared in the light of discussions in the Tripartite Working Party on the Police Act 1964* and with Chief Officers. It replaces Home

---

*The Tripartite Working Party comprises representatives of the Home Office, the Association of Chief Police Officers, the Association of County Councils and the Association of Metropolitan Authorities.

Office Circular No 232/1971 (Establishment Reviews and Forecasts of Strength) and 75/1979 (Police Expenditure — Civilianisation).

2. Since the 1971 Circular was issued the demands on the police have increased substantially. The number of serious crimes recorded by the police has practically doubled, while other commitments, such as the maintenance of public order, have also become more onerous. At the same time, police strength has increased substantially. Since 1971 police strength (excluding civilians) has gone up by some 24,000 and on 31 March 1983 there were 121,003 police officers in England and Wales. Expenditure has also increased substantially and the cost of the police service in 1982-1983 was £2.4 billion as compared to £1.4 billion in 1970-1971 (estimated at current prices). After this rapid growth a period of consolidation is desirable, not least because the constraints on public expenditure at both central and local government levels make it impossible to continue with the sort of expansion which has occurred in recent years. Yet the workload shows no sign of diminishing. If the police service is to deal with this situation and retain public confidence it is essential that it should make the most effective use possible of the substantial resources now available to it. This circular is intended to assist Chief Officers and Police Authorities to enhance police effectiveness in that context.

Establishments

3. It is against the background of resource constraints mentioned above that the Home Secretary has to consider applications for increase in police establishments. Although improved recruitment means that all forces are now able to operate at full establishment level, applications for increases, some of them quite large, continue to be received. It is impossible to approve them all, and the Home Secretary, advised by HM Inspectors of Constabulary, has to form a judgment about which should be given approval and with what priority. There is of course no standard formula that can be used to arrive at the appropriate establishment for a force: each application must be considered on its merits, taking account of local needs and circumstances. But this circular offers guidance on the criteria which the Home Secretary will have in mind.

4. Four general criteria will in future govern the Home Secretary's assessment of bids for increases in establishments. First, he will not normally be prepared to authorise additional posts unless he is satisfied that the force's existing resources are used to best advantage. He will look to HM Inspectors for their professional assessment of whether, for example, resources are directed in accordance with properly determined objectives and priorities,

and whether civilian manpower and technical support are effectively freeing police officers for operational duties. Second, it will not be sufficient for applications to be cast in general terms: a specific case for additional posts will need to be made. Third, no additional posts will be authorised unless the Police Authority (in consultation with the county council, as necessary) has signified its intention to fund them. Finally, increases will only be approved if they are to take effect in the current and/or in the immediately following financial year. Chief Officers and Police Authorities might find it helpful to develop their manpower planning over a longer period and the Home Secretary will so far as possible take long-term plans into account in considering individual applications for increases in the current and/or immediately following financial year; but since Government expenditure plans are reviewed each year additional resources for planned future increases in manpower cannot be committed more than a year ahead.

5. The Home Secretary will not normally be prepared to approve increases in establishment if police officers are occupying posts which could properly and more economically be filled by civilians. If in such cases an increase in manpower is necessary, priority should be given to the recruitment of civilians, to do the work at less cost and to release police officers for operational duties where their training and experience can be used to best effect. It should be noted that the levels of civilians recommended in previous Home Office Circulars (the last of which was No 75/1979) are no longer relevant and should be disregarded. It is recognised that in some areas the policy of civilianisation may run into difficulties because of the effects of present controls on local authority expenditure. Separate consideration is being given to this problem by the Tripartite Working Party.

Objectives and Resources
6. The last few years have seen changes not only in the resources available to the police but also in the demands made on them, both in traditional police work and in developing fields such as crime prevention and community relations. If scarce resources are to be deployed to the best effect in this changing situation it is important that Chief Officers and Police Authorities should have clear objectives and priorities, which themselves will change from time to time. The Home Secretary therefore attaches importance to the determination of objectives and priorities in the police service, and to the allocation of resources and the deployment of police and civilian manpower in a way that will most effectively and efficiently secure those objectives and priorities. (He recognises, of course, that major unforeseen developments will occur from time to time, and that resources

will need to be diverted, perhaps temporarily, to the immediate pressing problem.)

7. Many Chief Officers have already taken the initiative in consultation with their Police Authorities in carrying out major reviews of policies and consequently of the allocation of manpower and other resources. HM Inspectors of Constabulary have been encouraging reviews of this kind, and have been able to assist in them. Some forces which have undertaken such reviews have made significant shifts in their resources and by ensuring that police manpower is deployed at the times and in the areas where it is most needed, for example by changes in beat and shift patterns, have increased their effective operational strength without increases in establishment. Since demands and pressures change, there is clear need for such reviews to be carried out regularly, so that areas in which effort needs to be concentrated or reduced can be identified and resources switched to meet changing priorities.

8. The Police Authority has an important role to play in contributing to the formulation and review of the framework of objectives and priorities within which the force operates. In order to carry out its statutory duty of securing an adequate and efficient force, it will need to concern itself not only with questions of resources, but also with the needs and wishes of the local community. While the direction and control of the force remain the responsibility of the Chief Officer, it is necessary for the Police Authority and the Chief Officer to work together to ensure that the objectives and priorities which they determine are both founded on sound professional judgment and best calculated to reflect the wishes and needs of the public they serve. In addition, they both have an important responsibility to ensure that their policies are understood and accepted by the community as well as the force. The Home Secretary is concerned that the Police/Community Consultation machinery, on which guidelines were issued in Home Office Circular 54/1982, should be utilised to the full as a means both of determining local needs and wishes and of explaining policies publicly.

9. It is essential that the policing objectives should be understood by all ranks and expressed in terms which relate to the experience of more junior officers. Supervisory officers at all levels should be in a position to explain to the officers and civilian staff for whom they are responsible what is expected of them. Conversely the views and experience of more junior officers can make an important contribution towards the formulation of policy, and should be a valuable resource to the Chief Officer or the local

commander who is considering or reviewing his aims and objectives; the Edmund-Davies Committee in Part III of their Report recommended consultation not only through the force Joint Negotiating and Consultative Committee but also at Divisional level, and the use of working parties as a method of consultation through the operational chain of command.

10. The effective and efficient use of resources also depends crucially on knowledge of where and when they are most likely to be needed and what results they will have. In general resources should be applied on the basis of what they are likely to achieve. Chief Officers may wish to consider whether the management information that is necessary for informed decisions to be taken about the deployment of resources in accordance with the force's priorities and objectives has been properly identified. It is important to ensure not only that the information available at sub-divisional, divisional or force level meets the requirements of the appropriate level of command, but also that it is presented in an effective and manageable way, and that significant changes and trends are identified and brought to attention as soon as possible.

11. The potential demands on the police are such that they could not be met solely by increases in police strength, even if substantial additional resources were available. It is necessary to work in co-operation with other public services, voluntary bodies and the public themselves. Crime prevention, for example, on which a separate circular will be issued shortly, deserves a high priority in the general strategy against crime; it extends not only to the provision of locks and bolts, but also to environmental planning, to influencing the attitudes of children, young people and their parents, and to identifying and engaging with groups who may be particularly at risk, whether as offenders or victims. In drawing up their objectives and reviewing the allocation of their resources Police Authorities and Chief Officers should have this extra dimension in mind. They should also take account of the resource implications of using police officers in fields which are not traditionally the primary responsibility of the police.

12. Experience has shown that a number of potentially useful initiatives and experiments involving the redeployment of resources have run into the ground through inadequate preparation. In order to assess whether a new scheme is more successful than the arrangements which it replaced, a firm basis for comparison is necessary. This means that there must be information about, and analysis of, the old arrangements and a reasonable amount of time needs to be set aside for preparing the ground in this

way. Some experience in research techniques is helpful, and if only limited experience of that kind is available in the force the Chief Officer and the Police Authority may wish to consider seeking advice elsewhere. The Home Office itself contains a considerable degree of research expertise, including that at the Police Staff College, and would be able to offer advice as necessary. Forces are asked to consult HM Inspector in the first instance and to keep the Police Research Services Unit (PRSU) informed of their initiatives and experiments.

13. It is desirable that the experience gained in forces should be disseminated more widely, so that good practice can be spread and mistakes avoided. Chief Officers and their Police Authorities will also wish to look at experience elsewhere before embarking on initiatives of their own. This experience is disseminated in a variety of ways, such as Home Office Circulars, advice from HM Inspectors and the Information Desk of the PRSU, and informal contacts between officers of different forces. It is important that individual forces should contribute their own experiences to the common stock. For initiatives of major interest, this should be done by keeping HM Inspector informed. For mainly technical matters, forces are asked to pass any useful information to the PRSU Information Desk, who in turn will be glad to make information available to forces on request.

14. In a number of fields, such as equipment and training, facilities are available to forces nationally or regionally. At present, some forces prefer to make their own parallel arrangements rather than use the national or regional resource. Clearly this has implications not only for the particular force but also for the provision of the resource itself, and for other forces using it. Formal or informal co-operation between neighbouring forces, for example on training, may be more cost effective, and Chief Officers are invited to review their in-force arrangements with this in mind. It is important that HM Inspectors should be consulted; and they should be informed when any decision affecting the operation of collaborative arrangements is contemplated.

Inspections
15. The Inspectorate of Constabulary has a key role to play in enhancing police effectiveness and in helping to achieve the aims set out in this circular. HM Inspectors are now adopting in their inspections an approach which is more specifically directed towards the way in which Chief Officers, in consultation with the Police Authority and the local community, identify problems, set realistic objectives and clear priorities, keep those priorities and objectives under review, deploy manpower and other resources in

accordance with them, and provide themselves with practical means of assessing the extent to which Chief Officers are achieving their objectives. HM Inspectors' judgments about a force's effectiveness and efficiency will be based on this approach, as will their advice to the Home Secretary about any applications for increases in establishment. They will not attempt to prescribe identical methods in each force: their concern will be to ensure that each force has the necessary systems in place which will enable it to respond effectively, according to its local circumstances, to the particular demands placed upon it. In future years HM Inspectors will also be examining financial information and how costs are taken into account in considering the different options for deploying resources, and how value for money is ensured.

16. Inspections will bring out points relevant to a Police Authority's responsibility under section 4 of the Police Act 1964 for maintaining an adequate and efficient force and for providing buildings, vehicles, clothing and other equipment. It will be the usual practice for HM Inspectors to meet the Chairman and members of the Police Authority, with the Chief Officer, to discuss such issues. At the conclusion of an inspection, HM Inspectors will make a written report about such issues to the Police Authority with a copy to the Chief Officer.

Yours faithfully

D H J HILARY

Further Reading

J. Benyon and J. Solomos, *The Roots of Urban Unrest*, Pergamon, 1987

M. Castle and E. Gittus, 'The Distribution of Social Defects in Liverpool', *Sociological Review*, Vol 5, No 1, 1957

R. Dahrendorf, *Law and Order*, Hamlyn Lectures, Stevens & Sons, 1985

V.J. Donovan, *Christianity Rediscovered: An Epistle from the Masai*, SCM, 1978

D. Humphrey, *Police Power and Black Power*, Panther, 1972

M. Kettle and L. Hodges, *Uprising*, Pan, 1982

J. Lea and J. Young, *What Is To Be Done About Law and Order?*, Penguin, 1984

Liverpool Black Caucus, *The Racial Politics of Militant in Liverpool*, Merseyside Area Profile Group and the Runnymede Trust, 1986

P. Lloyd, *Slums of Hope*, Penguin, 1979

L. Lustgarten, *The Governance of the Police*, Sweet and Maxwell, 1986

J.B. Mays, *Growing Up In The City*, Liverpool University Press, 1954

E. Midwinter, *Priority Education*, Penguin, 1972

D. Sheppard and D. Worlock, *Better Together*, Hodder and Stoughton, 1988

S. Spencer, *Called to Account*, National Council of Civil Liberties, 1985

P. Wilding, *Professional Power and Social Welfare*, Routledge and Kegan Paul, 1982

Reports

Home Office, Circular 114, *Manpower, Effectiveness and Efficiency in the Police Service*, 1983

R. Kinsey, *Merseyside Crime Survey*, 1984

B. Loveday, *The Role and Effectiveness of the Merseyside Police Committee*, 1985

Merseyside Police Authority, *Interim Report of the Working Party on Police/Public Relationships*, 1981

Scarman, *Report of an Inquiry into the Brixton Disorders*, Cmnd 8427, 1981

SNAP 69/72, published by the Liverpool Project, 1972